# STOWE'S BIBI

# ASTROLOGY

## THE BIBLE FOUNDED
## ON ASTROLOGY
### (1907)

> **Contents: The Old Testament and Astrology or Religion Keeps Pace with the sun through the Great Zodiac; the Story of the Sun god and the Story of the Son of God are one and the Same; Man Made in the Image of His Creator, the Zodiac; The Riddle of the Sphinx Solved; The Seals of the Book of Revelation Broken.**

## Lyman E. Stowe

ISBN 1-56459-802-0

**Kessinger Publishing's Rare Reprints**
**Thousands of Scarce and Hard-to-Find Books!**

.        .        .
.        .        .
.        .        .
.        .        .
.        .        .
.        .        .
.        .        .
.        .        .
.        .        .
.        .        .
.        .        .
.        .        .
.        .        .
.        .        .
.        .        .
.        .        .
.        .        .
.        .        .

We kindly invite you to view our extensive catalog list at:
http://www.kessinger.net

*Yours Truly*

*Lyman E Stowe*

THE BIRTH OF THE SON OF GOD.

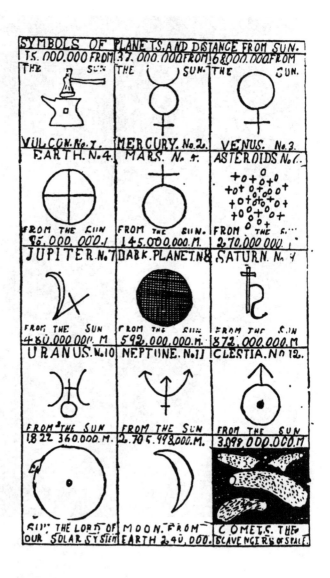

SYMBOLS OF PLANETS, AND DISTANCE FROM SUN.

| 15,000,000 FROM THE SUN | 37,000,000 FROM THE SUN | 68,000,000 FROM THE SUN |
|---|---|---|
| VULCON. No. 1. | MERCURY. No. 2. | VENUS. No. 3. |
| EARTH. N. 4. | MARS. N. 5. | ASTEROIDS No. 6. |
| FROM THE SUN 95,000,000.1 | FROM THE SUN 145,000,000. M. | FROM THE S. 270,000,000. |
| JUPITER. N. 7 | DARK PLANET. N. 8 | SATURN. N. 9 |
| FROM THE SUN 480,000,000. M | FROM THE SUN 592,000,000. M. | FROM THE SUN 872,000,000. M |
| URANUS. N. 10 | NEPTUNE. N. 11 | CLESTIA. No. 12. |
| FROM THE SUN 1,822,360,000. M. | FROM THE SUN 2,705,998,000. M. | FROM THE SUN 3,098,000,000. M |
| SUN THE LORD OF OUR SOLAR SYSTEM | MOON. FROM EARTH 240,000. | COMETS. THE SCAVENGERS OF SPACE. |

## THE TWELVE SIGNS OF THE ZODIAC.

Page I gives symbols of planets and 2 symbols of the signs of the Zodiac. Notice the three symbols of astrelogy, the circle, criscent and cross, are the baces of the symbols of all religeon as well as all other astrological symbols.

SYMBOLS OF THE SIGNS OF THE ZODIAC.

| SYMBOL OF | SYMBOL OF | SYMBOLS OF |
|---|---|---|
| SHORT LONG ARIES. | SHORT LONG TAURUS. | SHORT LONG GEMINI. |
| SYMBOL OF SHORT LONG CANCER. | SYMBOLS OF LONG SHORT. LEO. | SYMBOLS OF SHORT. LONG VIRGO. |
| SYMBOLS OF SHORT. LONG LIBRA. | SYMBOLS OF SHORT. LONG. SCORPIO. | SYMBOLS OF SHORT. LONG. SAGITTARUS. |
| SYMBOLS OF SHORT. LONG CAPRICORNUS. | SYMBOLS OF SHORT. LONG AQUARUS. | SYMBOLS OF SHORT. LONG PISCES. |

# INDEX TO BIBLE ASTROLOGY.

Page

Title Page ................................................

Preface ................................................

Copyright ................................................

The Twelve Signs of the Zodiac.....................1 to 30

Astrology and Phrenology ................................ 7

The Sun 2000 Years in a Sign............................ 9

More Than One Zodiac ................................... 9

The Earth's Change of Poles Brings Floods............... 9

When Thubin Was Pole Star.............................. 9

The Pyramids ........................................... 10

The Celestial, and Human Head.......................... 13

The Sun Has Now Entered Equarius—and What We May
    Expect ............................................. 14

Uranus Rules for a Thousand Years...................... 15

Man Made in the Image of the Creator ..................

The Zodiac ............................................. 17

Never Stops Snowing and Never Thaws at the South Pole. 18

The 49th Chapter of Genesis and the Twelve Signs of the
    Zodiac ........................................19 to 25

The Sign Gemini, the Garden of Eden.................... 25

The Zodiac on the Human Hand.......................... 28

The Christian Religion in the Movements of the Planets...28-29

The Circle, Half Circle, and Cross......................

The Symbols of All Religion............................. 29

And the Basis of the U. S. Flag—A God Given Country...to 40

The Origin of the Easter Festival....................... 40

God's Good Books ...................................... 45

The Birth of Eve or Mother Earth, From the Side of the
    Sun ............................................... 47

The Days of the Week Named After the Planets........... 47

20 Crucified Labor Leaders............................. 49

What a Wise Man Says.................................. 50

The Fight of All Reforms................................ 53

Parallels of Old Testament Passages and Truths in Astrology 54

God Everywhere, No Room for Anything Else, Man Evolved
    from God .......................................... 55

Reincarnation in the Bible ............................. 57

Astrological Time the Key to Bible Time................. 59

The Names of Jacob's Twelve Sons and Their Meaning..... 62

Stories of the Bible Made Plain by Astrology............ 68

Our Sunday Not of the Bible, But of Astrology........... 69

What is Meant by the Sin of Looking Backward.......... 72

God's Week—7000 Years ............................... 74

The Origin of Bull Worship............................. 74

The End of Jupiter's Rule and the End of the Rule of
    Wealth—One and the Same.......................... 76

Why We Have Socialism................................ 82

The Hardships of Jesus ................................ 85

The Setting Up of the Abomination That Maketh Desolate. 87

Why the Church Favors the King and the Millionaire...... 93

How Will It End?...................................... 97

The Meaning of the Man Bearing a Pitcher of Water...... 98

When Spiritualism is Strongest ......................... 101

Man Must Graduate to a Higher State................... 102

# INDEX TO BIBLE ASTROLOGY.

                                                              Page
The Twelve Signs of the Zodiac and the Twelve Sons of
  Jacob, One and the Same..........................101 to 103
The Riddle of the Sphinx.............................. 105
When Aquarius Begins to Reign........................ 116
The Story of the Sun God, and the Story of the Son of God 123
The Star of Bethlehem ............................... 125
The Story of the Sun God, and the Story of the Son of God
  Proper, or the New Testament........................ 128
Judas Iscariot, and the Betrayal...................... 133
Many Evidences Cited, Including Ecclesiastes, 3 Ch., That
  the Bible is Astrological............................ 138
The New Jerusalem—the New Zodiac to Aquarius Cycle... 141
What the New Jerusalem is Like....................... 148
The Sonnet to the Flag............................... 160
Closing Chapter—
Free Masonry and Astrology.....................166 to 190
The Astrologer's Belief or Creed..................... 194
Afraid of Freedom, the Words of a Wise Man........... 199
The Evolution of the Bible........................... 202
The Allegory of the Prodigal Son..................... 215
Why Sixty Seconds Make a Minute.................... 215
Astrology As a Science............................... 222

## ILLUSTRATIONS:

Birth of Christ ...........................................
Author's Picture .........................................
Symbols of Planets and Signs.............................
Twelve Signs of the Zodiac in Colors.....................   1
The Cosmic Man .........................................   2
Phrenological Heads .....................................   7
Astrological Head .......................................   8
Signs of the Hand.......................................  27
Religious Periods on the Zodiac..........................  66
The Sphinx ............................................. 105
The Sphinx from Another View........................... 107
The Interior of the Sphinx............................. 110
The Sphinx in the Zodiac............................... 118
The Son of God in the Zodiac........................... 123
Venus, the Star of Bethlehem........................... 125
The Three Wise Men..................................... 127
The Cross on Which the Sun is Crucified................ 130
The Second View of Cosmic Man......................... 135
The Sun ............................................... 140
Labor and Interest (Illustrated)....................... 156
Capital and Labor (Illustrated)........................ 157
Planet Jupiter ........................................ 193
The Clock and Signs of the Zodiac...................... 217
Cupid ................................................. 220
The Planets As They Rule the House.................... 221
Photo of Henry Clay Hodges ............................ 224
Photo of Frederick White .............................. 226
Photo of A. J. McDonald, M. D.......................... 227
A Scene by Moonlight................................... 228
Photo of Walter H. Lewis............................... 229
Father Time ........................................... 230

Bible Astrology is the outgrowth of conditions. I started to write a philosophical work, embracing the various phases of Astrology. My book grew to such proportions I was compelled to divide it into different departments. Astrology and the Bible became so prominent a part, I turned to the production of this volume, and yet much of the spiritual side of Astrology is to be found in my "Periodicity," $2.50, and in "Cosmos." 10 ctp

In the years gone by, I had met so much seeming organized conspiracy, or opposition, that I had about given up hopes of meeting with success, with any of my works, hence I got them up as cheaply as I possibly could, setting much of the type myself and I not a practical printer. I hoped only to leave records of truth, not generally known, that others might take up and improve on.

I feel sure my little book, the "Cosmos," will brush away many of the cobwebs, that cover the doorway of the future state, and this book and "Periodicity" will nail those truths fast in the mind of the readers.

I do not know which book bigoted people will dislike most.

"Astrological Periodicity," as its name implies, deals with the periods of life of persons, animals, times, and things, and should be treasured in every family as an indispensable guide to every-day life, to show how to take advantage of good periods and avoid evil ones, and the price $5.00 with charts, or $2,50 without, seems large, no person once in possession of the knowledge it teaches would be without it, and yet it, too, teaches much of this same philosophy.

I found many people who had read one or the other of these works were often recommending them and a cheap work was in demand as an introductory, hence my            book, the "Cosmos," which answers those three great questions, "Where did we come from? What are we here for?, and Where are we going to?"

Thinking people are singing its praises and I assure all lovers of truth, they will find my corrected "Bible Astrology" is but one of the series of books every person should read.

The book, "What is Coming?" is in the same line, though leading along the subject of finance. Price $1.50, in cloth; $1.00, paper.

The reason these works are spoken of in this Preface is, that the student along these lines may know where to get a more extended knowledge of the subject. I might add my "Poetical Drifts of Thought," $2.50, as it deals with world building and evolution.

Though I found the Bible an astrological work or astrology in allegory, I found so much prejudice against the word "Astrology," that some editors prefer not to advertise my works under that title, yet the first edition of my "Bible Astrology" is exhausted, without advertising, and so I am correcting the plates, revising, and correcting the original work, and hope to get it in the hands of every lover of truth.

The reader of this or that book may ask, what evidence I have that I am right, more than the theologians and historians of the past?

When Pilate asked Christ what is truth, it is said Christ held his peace.

When Napoleon was asked, "What is history?" he replied, "A lie generally accepted as truth."

All history, including the Bible, if subject to close criticism, will reveal many evidences of deception and error. All ordinary theology is based upon the Bible or other very weak testimony and very much on nothing stronger than a little philosophical imagination. While the history I see fit to quote is backed up by reasonable comparisons, and my theory by manifest effects of the everlasting heavenly bodies, whose testimony any good astrologer can summon at will, so I think I have a decided advantage over all other historians and theologians, and I am sorry this little work is not large enough to hold all of the subject desirable, and so I must refer the reader to the other works mentioned.

I did not think of writing a word on economic subjects, that came as a necessity to explaining the meaning   of the end of the world, or end of the Pisces world, or Sun's passover into Aquarius, in the great Zodiac or Recession of the Equinox.

I really do not like to find fault with my fellowman, for the reason that astrology teaches me to be lenient, as we all have faults.  Yet it is our duty to point out mistakes and wrongs wherever we find them.

If it had been my design to find fault with the church or economics, I could have made out such an array of facts that the work would have bristled with them.  But I have no desire to be severe unless attacked, though I know this work is likely to bring some hot replies.

However, this I will say, my knoweldge of Astrology tells me our present system of religion is destined to be wiped out, and unless the privileged class and the grafters make their peace with the people, their property will be confiscated and many of them will lose their lives, and the quicker they begin to balance up matters the easier will be the change and end.

I am ready to take any reformer by the hand, and to give credit where credit is due, be it in o r outside of the church, and any reader of this book who does not understand or thinks I do not understand, I say "Let us reason together."

**1**

THE ZODIAC, AND STORY AMONG THE STARS.
AND SECOND COMING OF CHRIST.

# The Author's Second Preface.

No man is perfect; it seems that all books must be revised one or more times, especially those of deep research.

My first attempt at book making was "Poetical Drifts of Thought," written in 1884, a work on world building and evolution.

This though from a materialistic standpoint is the clearest, most comprehensive book on the subject.

The author afterwards finding that mind and matter were one and the same thing, brought out his three lectures entitled "Cosmos," a 50-cent book.

This led the way to the discussion of the Bible; yet as the author was much interested in the financial question, it seemed out of place to dig into ancient lore, where the time should be spent for suffering men of today.

This led also into Bible study, hence in 1895, while assistant editor of the People's Paper, the author brought forth his "What Is Coming," which leads down to the present war.

The author, being an old soldier himself, found an easy task in connecting all the links of the past, present and future together.

Still one more element led to the research along the lines of spiritual phenomena, that on linking the subject of Bible Astrology with that of biblical and phenomenal history, that all four of the mentioned books are closely linked together.

Many clairvoyant meetings were indulged in, one of which was related here following the picture of the Godhead.

And believing they would be interesting to the public here for the following reason:

The great war having caused the rise in prices beyond all reason, it became necessary to raise the price of "Bible Astrology." This book was sold too low at $1.00, anyway, when so expensive and large a chart is given with the book, which is not generally taken into consideration by the purchaser; while $1.50 is very reasonable for such a book, with so grand and beautiful and expensive chart and additional matter here given.

"Visions on the Battlefield" and stories related of a trip through space with a celestial sweetheart that caused the author to determine to spread it broadcast, probably at $2.00 bound in cloth, as many numbers have been sent out as feelers, which has created a universal demand for the book.

Let me say that "Poetical Drifts of Thought" is an octave in size, well illustrated and beautifully bound Price $2.50 while this edition lasts. "What Is Coming" is a book of nearly 500 pages now, revised edition, with two charts 12x14 inches. Price, manila $1.00; cloth $1.50. While "Cosmos" is but a pamphlet it is the liveliest pamphlet the reader ever got hold of at 50 cents.

"Poetical Drifts of Thought," predicting the present war 35 years ago, even drawing the pictures of the flying machine and machine guns now in use.

The above picture is reproduced from a drawing shown in Practical Drifts of Thought, published in 1884.

Reduced size of cut reproduced here is illustration in Poetical Drifts of Thought; a table book; octavo in size; large type; bound in green and gold; containing many illustrations. Price $2.50. A prediction of the present great war of today.

"The flying machine would have been invented and successfully used long before this, if it were not for the danger attending the first attempt at flight, and which will be overcome at least to a great extent, as man becomes a little familiar with the new mode of navigation."—This is a quotation from "Poetical Drifts of Thought," published by Lyman E. Stowe in 1884.

THE FLYING MACHINE OF THE NEAR FUTURE.

This picture is reduced in size.

**NOTICE!**

I want it distinctly understood that I am not discussing the merits or demerits of this war, it had to be, or it would not have been predicted by me so many years ago.

# THE TWELVE SIGNS OF THE ZODIAC.

The zodiac effects all organic boddies, animate or inanimate. As an example look to the dates on the diagram, nearest your own date of birth, then turn to the same in the back of the book.

The zodiac is a circle of 360 degrees divided into 12 parts of 30 degrees each, through which our solar system revolves. It is com-

## THE TWELVE SIGNS OF THE ZODIAC.

posed of stars in constellations named the same as the signs of the Zodiac which once corresponded with them. This band extends from 8 to 9 degrees each side of the Ecliptic. somewhat zigzag, because some of the stars lay farther from the center of the line than others. The influence is produced by the vibrations the stars set up at the time of the birth or creation of any organized body which chances to be brought into existence under the direct rays of the sign or constellation as the earth passes from one sign to another during the different periods of the year. See diagram above.

The Zodiac is an imaginary zone or band through which our solar system revolves. It is a circle of 360 degrees, divided into 12 signs of 30 degrees each. The affect of the signs differ at different dates and through planetary positions (see diagram above). The quarter of love means that those born in that quarter are affectionate and lovers of home and domestic life. The quarter of wisdom means that those born in this quarter make much of education and look up to educated people and strive to educate their children. The quarter of wealth means that those born in this quarter make much of wealth and are

## THE TWELVE SIGNS OF THE ZODIAC.

generally dickerers or traders. The quarter of labor means that these people are active, must be on their feet, and are best adapted to business where great activity is requisite.

The domains are Fire, Earth, Air and Water, and they rule the temper. Those born in the fire signs are of high temper, even dangerous when fully aroused, but easily satisfied, and not revengeful. People of the Earth signs sulk a little, even when outspoken, but do not generally hold revenge. People of the Air signs are quick of temper, flashy, and quick over it, and easily overcome their temper, and are seldom rash. People of the Water signs vary in temper and nearly always hold a grudge until they get even. If they forgive even, the memory of the injury will never down.

The quality of domains run alternately from Aries to the left—mental, vital, neutral. The mental signs mean that the mind is too strong for the body, and where two mentals marry, the child must be physically trained, or the body will be too weak to sustain it. The vital signs show stronger physical power, and quick to recuperate from any form of ill health. The neutral signs show a balance in mental and

## THE TWELVE SIGNS OF THE ZODIAC.

physical forces and a reservation in expression of feelings of like and dislike. The tables below give the effect of the signs on the general health and character. Those born on the cusp or line between two signs are changeable in likes and dislikes, and partake of both signs

People generally agree best together who are born in the same sign, or in polars, opposite signs, or in the same domains, which are trion to each other.

Thus Aries and Sagitarius are trion fire signs. So the fire signs are trion and the water signs are trion and the earth signs are trion. Thus fire and water make steam, and an explosion. Earth and water makes mud, the air lashes the water to foam. Fire scorches the earth, and air blows up the fire more fierce; while the air drys up the earth. Sometimes people of opposing domains get along well together, because they have the same rising sign, or the same ruling planet, and sometimes they may seem to get along when the inner life is h—l. But it is best to marry in trions or polars.

The time of day or houses and planetary positions are what makes the greatest difference between people born of the same sign.

## The twelve signs of ehe zodiac.

More people marry their polars or trions than anywhere else.

To find the sign you were born in, look for dates at the lines dividing signs, and whichever date your birth comes between is your sign, then the corresponding figure at the head of descriptive matter of each sign is your fortune of Zodiacle horoscope.

### General instructions for care of children.

A person's stomach is the best moderator as to kind of food that is best for him. If possible let a child have what its stomach craves for, but limit the quantity, never letting a child over-feed.

Give children plenty of sleep, but get them up as soon as awake, and it is better that they sleep alone. You cannot guard a child too closely against the development of abnormal sex passions and self-abuse.

It is an old saying, "You spare the rod and spoil the child," but the father of that saying had no soul, and was only fit to keep wild beasts. It is a well-known fact you cannot train even domestic animals by the use of a whip, but kindness will conquer everything. If you must punish a child, do it by keeping from it some desired pleasure and teach it to sub-

## THE TWELVE SIGNS OF THE ZODIAC.

mit to reason, and above all, reason yourself, and see that you do not exact unreasonable things. But don't show anger, don't strike, don't whip.

# THE COSMIC MAN.

Head and Face. ARIES, The Ram.

Arm. GEMINI, The Twins.

Neck. TAURUS, The Bull.

Heart. LEO, The Lion.

Breast. CANCER, The Crab.

Reins. LIBRA, The Balance.

Bowels. VIRGO, The Virgin.

Thighs. SAGITTARIUS, The Bowman.

Secrets. SCORPIO, The Scorpion.

Legs. AQUARIUS, The Waterman.

Knees. CAPRICORNUS, The Goat.

Feet. PISCES, The Fishes.

The above cut showes, without further comment, the part of the body is effected by each sign of the Zodiac. No surgical operation should be permitted when tne Moon is in the sign represnting that part of the body wherein the disease is located.

It should also be rembered that the patient will be worse the days the Moon transits the sign of the body in which the disease is located.

## ASTROLOGY AND PHRENOLOGY, OR THE ZO-

## DIAC AND THE HUMAN HEAD.

It is said man is made in the image and likeness of his creator. To thoroughly understand this we must understand that in the embryo or fetus, the human form lies in a circle, the feet double to the head. The Zodiac, a circle, is his creator.

Now look at the accompanying cut and you will see that Phrenology and Astrology teach the same things in a slightly different way.

The Phrenologist points to the measurements of the head to show where the various functions lie. while the Astrologer points to the Zodiac to show where the greatest influence lies that put the bumps, or functions, where they are.

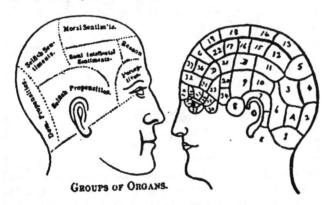

GROUPS OF ORGANS.

Look at the little Phrenological cut of the human head and note the number of figures above the eyes; that is where the perceptives lie.

Now look at the Asrtological head surrounded by
the Zodiac and note that Aries, the first mental sign,
is at the head of the Zodiac, or the first sign from
which all Astrological calculations are made, and the
perceptives, or bright, brain powers are calculated
from that point.   The description of the influence
of the Zodiac will aid in a more perfect understanding of this subject.   Bible writers veiled this story
in their allegory of Creation.

The Sun in his great Zodiac passed through the
12 signs of the Zodiac once every 26,000 years, and
civilization is blotted out and rebuilt twice in that
length of time.

I make this the opening chapter that the student of human nature may better understand how and why man is made as he is. That the destiny of man is the design of an intelligent creator is clearly manifest to the deep student of Astrology.

While this chapter properly belongs in the book, "The Spiritual Side of Astrology," and the first half of it will reappear there, it is necessary to give it in "Astrological Periodicity" that the student of human nature may better understand how and why man is made as he is. That man is the work of an intelligent creator is manifest in the great Astrological plan so clearly seen by the deep student of the Zodiac and its effects on all life and all mundane affairs.

As shown, the Sun is a little over two thousand years in each sign, while transiting its great circuit.

As the Sun is 2,000 years in a sign and the Earth but one month in a sign, while the Earth is but 95,000,000 of miles from the Sun, it cannot be the same Zodiac, or else we cannot be talking of it in the same sense.

As explained elsewhere, it is the same Zodiac which centers on every body, so as the Sun was 2,000 years in the sign Pisces, the Earth was with the Sun receiving the entire influence of Pisces as it focused upon the Sun, and every year receiving the special influence of Pisces from February 19th to March 21st, while these are effected by the changing vibrations (see chapter on vibration in "Astrological Periodicity") caused by the changing position of the planets or Sun's satellites. .

The Earth changes its poles every 13,000 years; thus for 13,000 years Aries stands at the head of the Zodiac, and for the other 13,000, Libra stands at the head; this will be better understood by reading the chapter in "The Spiritual Side of Astrology" entitled "The New Jerusalem and the effects of precious stones on man." Thus Thubin was the Pole Star until about 2,500 years ago.

That ancient Astrologers understood this is proven by the fact that the pyramids and the Sphinx were built to preserve the evidence of these truths. Six of the largest pyramids of Egypt were so erected that their tombs, or openings by which was the only way they could be entered, pointed, when erected, to Thubin, then Pole star. That is, when erected, Thubin could be seen from the interior of the tunnel, and interior of the pryamids.

That these ancient Astrologers understood, not only Astrology but Astronomy, is shown by the fact that Julius Caesar employed his wise men of Chaldea to correct the time tables, and they figured the winter solistic to the minute, and no mathematician has ever been able to add or to take from one proposition of Euclid of 2,500 years ago. But the scientific relics like the corrected calendars, the structors like the pyramids. Even the shape of the coast of Africa, itself, all go to prove a greater knowledge of science, in all of its forms, than we have at present.

That the Pyramids were erected on scientific principles of high order and for a great purpose, of which we have not yet discovered, is shown by not only what has been discovered of what they represent as well as the locality they occupy.

Commencing with the year 1843, and for several years, and even to the present time there were many societies going in body to Palestine and Egypt investigating those old historic wonders. Even the officers of the various national navies, when performing their annual evolutions, met in those waters for unusual studies. Finally on one occasion, when the officers of several ships were dining together, an American lieutenant called attention of his fellow-officers to the fact that the eastern coast of Africa was a perfect semi-circle. This, remember, is the Astrological symbol of the Moon and the symbol of the religion of a third of the people of the religious world. This lieutenant suggested that a survey be made from the two horns or ends of this semi-circle inward to a point square or at right angles, where he thought something unusual would be found.

The survey was finally made, and at exactly the point the pyramid Cheops, the largest of the structures, was found. This was evidence, the pyramids were built for some great scientific purpose and by people wise enough to take advantage of that locality, shaped by the hand of God or nature, or else created, by that great wisdom, in that shape to serve some great religious or scientific purpose, for here we find the part the circle, half circle and square plays in the affairs of man.

Upon examining the pyramids it is found it tells its own latitude, the true shape of the earth, the true length of its polar axis; the distance of the Sun. The law of gravitation; the density of the Earth; the days in the year; the length of the precessical cycles; gives a standard of weights and measures. squares, the circle, and gives so many Masonic symbols that a noted Free Mason declared, it is "The Keystone to the lost art, which interprets the grand science of living as a Masonic Lodge. For ages it has been the rejected stone. The world has not known it and the builders of science have thrown it away amidst the rubbish of speculative possibilities. It is a veritable lodge of Free Masonry."

Undoubtedly these structures were built to preserve evidence of the former high state of civilization, by preserving relics of their science and the ancient religion and Free Masonry, their highest social society, both of which have fallen so far into decay that they are mere pastimes and instruments of the rich to control the poor, and must either be purified or pass into decay and death. They must all go with the exclusiveness of a false competitive system and false idea of divine right of Kings and a robbing wage or salary system, which gives the highest wages to the person of most influence, a system of social and political privilege of robbery, belonging to the Pisces period. Though the pyramids were built at the flood period, which occurred about 9,000 years ago, and which destroyed Atlantas and the greater part of the civilized world.

The next great flood will occur when the Sun, in the great Zodiac, passes through Capricornus to Sagittarius—in about 4,000 years.

It is the Sun passing through the signs of the Zodiac and remaining in each sign over 2,000 years, while the Earth and other planets are continually moving, that constitute the laws of evolution, and raise man from sleeping soul atoms in Earth, through evolution and re-incarnation, through vegetation and animal life or lives, to a worthy state in spirit life; and it is this process of Zodiacal influence on which we are now treating. Each two thousand years must bring general different conditions, because the Solar system, which of course includes our Earth, were under so much different conditions, when our system was passing through Gemini, it was in a neutral air sign, the first of the intellectual quarter, representing a point in the human head which represents love of intelligence and love of home, yet love of travel and a very restless condition. Thus all things brought to life in this sign are influenced strongly by it, are restless and rebellious, yet easily controlled. (See description of each of the signs of the Zodiac.)

Right opposite Gemini in the crown of the head is the sign Sagittarius, which strongly influences religious matters. In these positions in the human head we frequently point to the faculties ruling these matters.

The sign Gemini represents the period spoken of in Genesis as the Garden of Eden, which really means the spirits called Gods were assisting mankind on Earth. But as the Sun went out of Gemini into Taurus, the Sun had passed its polar and the Earth was drawing away from the influence of Thubin, the then Pole star, so when the Sun passed out of the sign Gemini into the vital sign Taurus, it changed the nature of animal life and made man more animal, and less spiritual. Remember Taurus is in that part of the celestial head covering the part of the phrenological faculties of Alimentiveness, or love of eating and drinking. This is the polar of Scorpio, which rules the privats, secrets and rectum, all of those animal functions of a low order and most noticeable in lower animal nature, causing man to rebel against the higher nature and against the instructions of the rulers of Gemini. But civilization was destroyed by the flood, which came by the change of Earth's poles which was gradually taking place with the change of the Pole star Thubin to Polarius.

The Sun finally entered Aries, the sign of the Lamb. Or period of Christ.

Look at the cut of the Zodiac representing the celestial, or God head, and you find right at the bridge of the nose, or Aries and Pisces, all Astronomical and Astrological calculations are made, and by Phrenology all of the perceptives are found. (See Phrenological head.)

The polars of these two signs are Libra and Virgo. In Astrology, Libra rules marriage and Virgo rules maternity.

The 49th chapter of Genesis, where Jacob blesses his 12 sons, he is really giving the effects of the 12 signs of the Zodiac on those born under the sign, or where they cast their influence, just as the nature of the gems given to the gems of which are asigned to the 12 gates of the Celestial City, which is the Zodiac. (See article on Celestial City.

It has been stated that Libra was once the first sign of the Zodiac and Jacob assigned Rubin, his first born, to this sign, while Aries has taken the place of Libra ,and Gad, the seventh son, has taken the place of Rubin, and Libra people have ever since shown they are subject to spells of great despondency or sadness because of the loss of position.

While Aries people, or people born between March 21st and April 19th, though extremely lamb-like and forgiving, are as hard and cutting as the diamond, the stone that represents them, like the ram, when angered, they are dangerous.. Yet they are the overcomers.

Since Christ, a period of wonderful planetary influence, the Sun has been passing through Pisces in its great Zodiac.

Pisces is the polar of Virgo, which is the first sign of the maternal quarter, as Pisces is the first sign of the serving quarter; thus these two signs exert great domestic influences—Virgo as the maternal or mating influence, and Pisces the virtue of taking care of the family. Jupiter is the Lord of this sign, hence we have the rule of money for the past 2,000 years. But the Sun has entered the serving quarter and there is a strong tendency of mankind to be religious and serve God, hence it is called the serving quarter.

The Sun has now entered Aquarius, called the highest and lowest of all of these signs. It is the most spiritual of all the signs; it is presided over by the great spiritual planet Uranus, who is nearest in effect to the influence of the Sun. Hence is called the Son of the Sun God.

Note Aquarius is the polar of Leo, right opposite which is presided over by the Sun, or life giver. The Lion of the 12 signs of the Zodiac or tribes of Judah. Just as I have pointed out, Pisces representing the feet opposite to the head, though not the polar of Aries, I have pointed out that all of the lower functions are the polars of the higher ones and in locality where Phrenology points as the seat, of alimentiveness, or love or eating and drinking, its polar shows the rectum and organs of lower order. Virgo contains the influence to love of mating and first of caring for the offspring. Pisces shows love of knowledge, hoarding wealth for a rainy day, and organizing society and serving thoughts of a higher order.

So the Sun having entered Aquarius, the sign that has not a star of the first magnitude in it and is ruled over by Uranus, which formerly had no house to lay his head. This, like the allegorical story of Christ, represents the justice or rule that is about to come to the people as the rule of money is about to pass away.

It will be noticed that in Phrenology that the organs representing amativeness and combativeness lie in the back of the head. It will also be noticed that Leo is the polar of the Spiritual sign Aquarius, and that Leo lies in the back of the Celestial head, and as these organs are the rulers or promoters of generation and protection of the offspring, so is the Sun, the Lord of Leo and life giver of all vegetable and animal organisms.

Great intellectual and spiritual advancements must take place while the Sun lingers in this sign, preceded by a reign of hypocrisy and social crimes caused by the tremendous influence of the polars of Aquarius and Capricornus and the powerful aspects of the Sun's satellites in those signs at that time; together with the relative position the Earth has assumed to the fixed stars at that time.

During 1,000 years, Uranus, a planet of the second octave, will rule in place of Jupiter, the God of wealth and Lord of Pisces, while the Sun is passing through the first half of Aquarius, Uranus is distinctly a reformer and planet of the people in a sign without a single star of the first magnitude, so there will be 1,000 years of as complete individual justice and lack of privilege as it is possible to be. Because Uranus is the Son of the Sun God, who gives freely to all. No respecter of persons, and Uranus reigns for 1,000 years, this is the millenium, the thousand years, Revelation says Satan, Saturn is to be bound and then loose'd for a season to deceive the nations. How deceive the nations? Why, Saturn assumes its selfish competitive satanic influence.

Why are these effects attributed to Saturn? Because Saturn is of the nature of the fixed stars ruling a part of Aquarius and the sign Capricornus, which rules honor, dishonor and business. The Sun will have passed through that part of Aquarius giving justice to all and entered the influence of Capricornus, by which we judge business honor and dishonor. What is the perfect nature of Capricornus people? It is a strong sense of duty or conscientiousness. Where is this bump found in the human head? Right in the top of the head, isn't it? Now look at the Celestial or Zodiacal head, and you find this sign that produces these effects. When perverted, selfishness and trickery take their place.

The ancients saw this resemblance to the human head, hence said: "Man is made in the image and likeness of his creator, which must be an intelligent power." This being the case, man must be put on this Earth for a purpose. What is that purpose? Could it be anything else but experience, a school?

Thus the circle represents the sun, the life giver, the father. The half circle spirituality; the Moon, the Mother and indulger. The Cross, the trials and tribulations that man must bear the cross in the circle, the symbol of the Earth with the spirituality of the Moon and influence of the planets to help him to progress and the necessity of reincarnation, every 2,000 years, or thereabouts, every time the Sun changes from one sign to another in the great Zodiac.

We found the air sign Gemini, we called the Garden of Eden. A period of rest. In the intellectual quarter, we haven't dropped the intellectuality, but we advanced into the quarter of spirituality and into the serving quarter, a higher order of intellectuality, and on reaching Pisces, the beginning of the quarter, we found the influence of Virgo mating strong; this is the polar of Pisces and we find the higher order of the same principle extremely active; that is, a desire to save for the benefit of the family; so as Pisces is ruled over by Jupiter, the God of wealth, the past 2,000 years have been that of money worship.

As the influence is strongest when a planet is going out of a sign into the next, we have had and will have a stronger expression as the Sun left Pisces and enters Aquarius. So we may now look for greater expressions of selfishness and money-grasping on the part of the trusts, also more licentiousness and expressions of the lower passions, such as alamentiveness or over-eating and drinking, and its natural correlary amativeness and expressions of lower passions with combativeness—prize fighting, contentions in family, church and state. In fact, have we not had it for several years? This will be overcome by true spirituality, wisdom, reason and common sense. These faculties are located in the fore part and the upper part of the head, as the signs Aries, Pisces, Aquarius and Capricornus, the signs that beget these faculties are located in that part of the Celestial head from eyes to crown of head.

After the mastery by the higher order of things, equality, justice and true spirituality, this condition reigns for a thousand years, while Uranus retains his power, representing the 1,000-year reign of Christ, when Saturn again influences man to what they term a higher individuality than can only be gained through the competitive system. This is the expression of honor, dishonor and business, so strongly manifest in Capricornus. It is Saten loosed for a season to deceive the nations, which means when the Sun finally enters Capricornus, matters will have settled to systematic conditions again, but still of the competitive system.

The spirit or soul of all of those fit to be taken to a higher sphere, leave this Earth will not have to come back, while the souls who have not graduated will have to remain while the Sun is passing through Capricornus. They are having a second chance, while those who do not then graduate must remain another 26,000 years, while the Sun makes another circuit. By the time the Sun enters Sagittarius, he has drawn the Earth so far around; Polarius has lost his power and the Earth tips over, causing the mountains of snow and ice of the South Pole to come under the Equator and melt so rapidly that the whole Earth is surrounded by a dense cloud of vapor, which acts like a wet blanket, keeping all of the heat under it and making the whole Earth a tropical clime.

We must remember that for many ages it has continued to snow at the South Pole and never thaw. This must pack to ice, until the mountains of ice are miles high above our heads. Something must become of it, and it of itself helps to unbalance the Earth and cause a more sudden and radical change when the time does come, though the poles will not change completely until the Sun has passed through the sign Scorpio, about 8,000 years from now. When the Sun passes out of Capricornus it will end this dispensation. Civilization will be about wiped out; in fact, nearly all animal life will be destroyed. The spirits of those that could graduate will go to a higher sphere; those who cannot will remain to form new bodies to repopulate the Earth and aid the soul atoms that now lie dorment and sleeping in mother Earth, but will then come up in plant life and vegetation will grow very rank and form new coal beds. That which we are now liberating from the coal will form

the insect and reptillion life, which is to take a higher
position later on.

The sign Sagittarius is a hot firey sign. This sign
and Scorpio produces the highest tempered people
of any sign of the Zodiac. It is from this sign we
judge religion or morals. As what population was
left on the Earth to repopulate it, together with the
Souls not allowed to graduate, could not help but
see they had not lived right, they would naturally become more obedient and willing to be led very
strongly impressed with religious morals, which the
sign still exerts on those born under it; or its influence. Besides we find Gemini, the Garden of Eden
its palor, exerting a similar influence. (See the
Eastern gate of the New Jerusalem in        · or
Bible Astrology.)

As Sagittarius causes veneration and love of religious matters, and its location in the Zodiac or
celestial head, we also find veneration in the top of
the phrenological head.

People born strongly under the influence of Sagittarius are the highest tempered, yet exceedingly religiously inclined. It was the tribe representing this
sign who were chosen as priests among the Jews.
So we find the bumps or attributes in the same position in the phrenological head that we found them
in the celestial head, showing the Zodiacal head the
eause and the phrenological head the location.

During the two thousand years the Sun is in this
sign the Earth is intensely hot, caused by the tremendous cloud of vapor from the melting ice which
has now come under the Equator. The clouds of
vapor hold the heat to earth and all animal life, including the few of mankind, are sweltering under
the terrific heat.

This is the hades where the worm dieth not, for such a condition is conducive to rapid growth of vegetable and first forms of insect and reptillion life. This is called the Reproducing quarter. The Earth is several thousand years changing its poles before Thubin becomes the Pole Star again. Meantime this condition is rapidly awakening the sleeping soul atoms of Earth and vegetation is arising so rapidly and falling back to fossilize into coal to furnish the fuel for future generations. So many of our people of the present day fear will be left without fuel. The soul atoms now composing vegetation and coal will develop into reptillion and insect life of future ages, while the lower animal life of today will develop into lower forms of mankind. (See Poetical Drifts of Thought," "The Universe" and Atomic Soul Theory.)

The Sun will have now passed through the water sign Scorpio and entered the air sign Libra. It must be remembered the water signs Pisces, Scorpio and Cancer are all fruitful signs, while the fire and earth signs are developing signs, the air signs are resting or harvesting signs. As Libra is a mental sign and the sign of the balance, there was rapid development in evolving the lower order of animal life to the higher life. The development is extremely rapid. Libra represents great love and affection. People born under the influence of Libra are very loving, but it is very apt to run to permiscuity A Libra man can love a dozen wives. Therefore this affection runs to amativeness, or animal passion. Now look to your phrenological head and you find the bumps of the animal passion in the back of the head, as I have explained before; so you see the sign that produces them are in the back of the celestial head or Zodiac.

I have called the Bible an Astrological work, and pointed to the fact that in the 49th chapter of Genesis, Jacob—in blessing his 12 sons—gives the attri-

butes of those born under the 12 signs of the Zodiac.
(to thoes interested in "Bible Astrology,") I must refer to my "Universe," "Cosmos," and "Periodicity."

To Libra, Rubin is assigned Genesis 49:3.

"Rubin, thou art my first-born, my might and the
beginning of my strength, the excellency of dignity
and the excellence of power."

Fourth verse: "Unstable as water, thou shalt not
excel because thou wentest up to thy father's bed;
then defiledst thou it."

In other respects Rubin proved to be the brightest
and most trusted of all of the 12 sons. See the New
Jerusalem in "Spiritual Side of Astrology."

But why was the first son chosen to represent the
seventh sign, or back of the head, instead of the
front or Aries, if the Zodiacal head has any connection with the phrenological head?

The answer is clear. When the Sun was passing
through Libra, Thubin was the pole star and Libra
was the ascendant. Hence the Helio-Centric system
is the oldest system of Astrology and the blessing of
the 12 tribes was by the Helio system.

Jacob takes his sons, by their age, going to Scorpio,
Sagittarius and Capricornus, then jumps over to
Cancer. The reason for this is made plain, in the
article in "Spiritual Side of Astrology" explaining
the 49th chapter of Genesis, but it is out of place
here.

Of course the changing of the poles made Aries
the ascendant or first sign of the Zodiac, which was
given to the seventh son—Gad.

Nineteenth verse: "Gad, a troop shall overcome
him; but he shall overcome at the last."

Every Astrologer knows that in describing Libra,
the seventh gate or angle of the beautiful city that
descends out of the heavens, the "New Jerusalem,"
is given the beautiful stone, the opal, called the un-

fortunate stone, while that given to Aries, the first gate, is the diamond, which is used to cut everything else because of its hardness, yet at first it is a little gray stone dug from earth. He also knows the Aries man's nature is combative and progressive, he is also called the overcomer. He also knows that people strongly influenced by the sign Libra are subject to frequent spells of sadness, as if they had met with a great loss.

Up to the time the Sun has passed from Capricornus to Virgo, it has been passing through the reproductive quarter, or quarter of wealth. Reproduction has been tremendous, but the poles of the Earth are again accumulating the moisture in snow and ice, which of course does not all remain, but large quantities of it break away and again comes under the equator, yet enough has been stored to allow of the cooling of Earth again and the coarser growth of vegetation and animal life gives way to the more refined, hence as the Sun enters the sign Virgo, it enters the maternal quarter and mateing becomes stronger; previous to that there was no mateing among the lower animal life and it was held very loosely among man as attributed to Rubin.

The question may be asked here, If Jacob was giving the attributes of the 12 signs of the Zodiac to the 12 tribes of Israel, how it comes that there was 12 tribes of Israel?

The question is easily answered by calling attention to the fact that Judea, Egypt, Chaldea, Babylon and all of the advanced nations were Astrologers and did everything by Astrology, even to marrying by Astrology. The Israelites carried it to such an extent that they formed tribes of their own people. Hence the tribe of Judea sprang from Judah, the fourth son, attributed to Capricornus. The goldstone is given to this gate and love of gold, avarice, is the chief attribute of the Jewish people to this day. But read elsewhere in these works the noble attributes that are effected by the influence of Capricornus: "I must do this because it is my duty."

After the Sun entered Virgo and that sign so strongly influenced the mateing desire and terrible influence, civilization began taking on a higher order and a desire to accumulate and to learn, showing the influence of Jupiter, the God of Wealth, and the influence of the opposite signs of the Zodiac, Aries and Pisces. Mercury, the God of Language and Trade, rules Virgo. This quarter is called the maternal quarter, or quarter of wisdom, and we find Virgo in the back of the Zodiacal head, same locality we find the bumps or organs governing maternity and love of home that we find in the Phrenological head.

After the lower nature has learned to love strong enough to desire one mate, or conjugality has come up high enough to desire one mate and protection of its offsprings, combativeness became necessary, to protect the home; this is found low down in the back of the Phrenological head, and the sign Leo is also found low down in the back of the Celestial head, opposite to the sign of spirituality ruled by Uranus, while Leo is ruled by the Sun. Thus it was understood the Sun is the life-giver, the father; while Uranus, right opposite, and the only planet which in Astrology has the nature of the Sun, was called the only begotten son of the father.

In Astrology Uranus was never until recently given a house, consequently, like Christ, had no place to lay his head.

While Aquarius, the spiritual sign, and Uranus, the spiritual planet, are helping man to a higher plain of spirituality, the laws of evolution are elevating vegetable and lower animal life by the law of attraction. The atoms on a higher plane attract those on a lower plane; thus the organs are built up and so the whole animal system. This increases amitiveness, which in turn increases the family, but if carried to excess destroys the physical system. Thus the warmth of the Leo sun builds and matures the growth of vegetable and animal life, but when you plant or try to cultivate during the month of August, which he rules and is strongest, you waste your seed and destroy that you try to build up.

The last sign to consider is Cancer, June 22nd to July 22nd—the last sign of the maternal quarter, or quarter of wisdom; that is, the last quarter coming from that direction, right opposite the spiritual sign Capricornus, where I pointed out conscientiousness lay. We also found this the dividing way. At the second trial, all that were fit to graduate went higher, the others had to go through the sad experience of repopulating the earth after the great catastrophe caused by the sudden change of the Earth's poles.

While the sign Cancer is a mental sign, producing more intellectual than physical beginnings and as a member of the maternal quarter pushing her children on to education, there is also a strong tendency to drift backward toward the animal. Thus where she influences she has a tendency to produce large families, hence it is the very best of the fruitful signs.

Notice Cancer is in the throat of the Celestial head; thus we notice wherever people born of a strong Cancer influence are liable to take to over-eating and drinking and if they do they seldom reform. When the Sun entered that sign these tendencies became so strong that under the law of the great eternal intelligence it became necessary to give the intelligent organic life of Earth some assistance; hence the spirits of those who had graduated when the Sun was in Aquarius to Capricornus came back to Earth and assisted all that would come into the Garden of Eden, Gemini, or the first sign of the intellectual quarter. Thus man was in the Garden of Eden about two thousand years. But this is the intellectual quarter, receiving its influence from the religious, repentent, hot, hellish sign Sagittarius. Thus people born under Gemini are restless, desirous of being on the go. Therefore, do not serve a domestic animal, or set a turkey, goose or hen when the Moon is in Gemini, for the offspring will be fretty and restless. You cannot keep it home unless penned up.

When the Sun went out of Gemini the people left the care of the spirits' and went out to learn for themselves. Thus you again travel the circuit of the Sun in its course around the great Zodiac. The Sun has entered Aquarius and we are about to get the milennium of one thousand years reign of Uranus, the son of the Sun God. "This is the end of the world," so often looked for, the Pisces world or Sun passing through the sign Pisces. This is the time when "the Stars of the Heavens shall fall to the Earth like a tree casting its untimely fruit shaken by a mighty wind." See Revelation. This of course could not be the Stars or the Suns so far distant it has taken 3,000,000 of years for their light to reach us. What is it, then? Why, just what it says— kings, princes and money-lords.

Again Revelation: "Every mountain and every island shall be moved out of its course." Can this mean the great Rocky chain, the Blue Ridge, the Andies, the Alps, and all of the rest? Certainly not. What would become of poor Mother Earth if such a thing should take place? What then can it mean? Why, governments, of course. Every government will change. The people will no longer pay such robbing salaries to kings and politicians. They will not longer allow themselves to be robbed by trusts, but will establish new forms of governments, for "every bondman and every freeman will cry out for the mountains and rocks to fall upon them and hide them." See Revelations.

This does not say every good man or every bad man, but everybody. Why will they want the mountains and rocks to fall upon them? Because if mountains and islands mean governments and new governments are to be formed to avoid present systems of robbers, municipal ownership and government ownership will take the place of present systems. Have we not got a good start? When this is fully under way, the individual cannot compete with governments and there will be nothing left for man to do but to cry out to the mountains and rocks—governments—to fall on him and hide him, give him work and protection. "Oh! give me a job, give me a job; I can't make a living outside of the government."

Of course the kings, money-loaners and trusts will not give up their soft snaps without a fight, so if they will do what has been proven they are doing, they will not hesitate to make war, so "blood will flow to the horse bridles."

That is, until the Sun passes into Aquarius to the neck of Pagausius, the constillations of the horse.

I have now shown the nature of all of the signs and their stronger influence when the Sun is passing through the signs. We will now notice what effect the Moon has upon vegetable and animal life.

I must, however, call attention to the statement that a part of the people went back during the Capricornus period. Cancer being opposite, the tendency is to go back and when the Sun was passing through Cancer the tendency of many of the people was to go back to animal life, hence the sign of the crab, a thing which crawls backwards.

Not only the Head receives the marks of the Zodiac, but the Hand and every part of the Body.

I will not go farther than to show that Palmistry like phrenology is astrological; this is best done by referring to the accompanying c u t , which shows on the mounts and the phalanges the signs of the Zodiac and the name of all the planets used in Geo-Centric astrology. Uranus rules the first two lines across the wrist. Neptune the other two. As these planets are especially noted for their great length of time in making their cir-

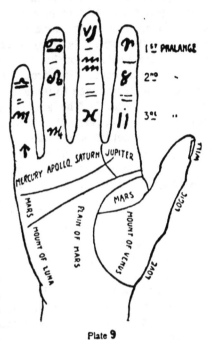

Plate 9

THE MOUNTS OF THE HAND.

cuit they should be used to designate the lines of the length of life. My "Secrets of Palmistry" explains all of this matter and this wonderful work, containing forty illustrations, mailed free for fifty cents.

Address Prof. Lyman E. Stowe, 131 Catherine St., Detroit, Mich.

## THE STORY OF THE CHRISTIAN RELIGION
## ENACTED BY THE SUN AND STARS
## EVERY YEAR.

Is it a proof of the truth of the Christian religion, or is it a proof all religion is myth, based upon astrology? If so, is this the reason the ministers are opposed to astrology? Do they fear astrology will expose a false position or have they so long been strangers to the occupation from which their title originated that they cease to understand the meaning of the word "divine"? The ancient priests were diviners (i. e.) astrologers; they became corrupt, preferring to serve selfish kings and politicians, as many of them do today, instead of serving God or the people, so they dropped astrology and substituted unknown tongues, to better and easier deceive the people.

As I can find no fault with the grand ideal character of Christ and do find astrology a great, good and truthful science, I prefer to believe both are, in some way, a part of God's great plan.

I find the Christian religion under a cloud to explain my findings to the public, especially since the church opposes astrology, I write this book.

Some people will say, "O this is too sacred a thing to tamper with."

I answer: He who will cover up an error or a lie under the pretense of a public good is a liar and an enemy to his God and to his fellow-man.

"Truth crushed to earth will rise again,
  The eternal years of God are hers;
While error wounded writhes in pain
  And dies amid her worshipers."

As for myself I love the ideal character of Christ,
and it pains me to think that for the sake of truth
I must prove the great character is but an allegory,
and prove that all religion is based upon ancient Sun
worship, and that in turn was based upon astrology.
I shall be pleased if any one is able to prove, without falsification, that I am wrong. But, they must
first read my other works before they can properly
understand my position.

If you will notice the signs of the Zodiac surround-
ing the cut of the Zodiac are called long signs, while
those below are called short signs; these are compos-
Jd of the circle, the half circle and the cross, short-
ened for rapidity of writing. All of these are older
than all other recorded history by thousands of years,
as they are found engraven on the pyramids and obe-
lisks of Egypt and on the temples of India, all of
which are older than other recorded history.

Astrology is older than the Bible because the Bible
speaks of it.

These are the short signs of the Zodiac, being made
up of the parts of the cross and the circle and the
half circle, which are symbols of all religion:

☉     ☾     ⊕

The cross is the symbol of the Christian religion
and stands for body, a load, a burden to bear. The
Sun god, like the allegorical Son of God, is crucified
on the great cross, consisting of the line through the
Earth, east and west, or March 21st and Sept. 23rd,
the spring and fall equinox, or when the days and
nights are of the same length. The long stem of the
cross running north to south, or December 22nd to
June 21st, the summer and winter solstice, or the long-
est and shortest days of the year. John the Baptist,
who was born six months before the Son of God, or
the Sun god, and he who said, "He must increase, I
must decrease."—John, 3rd chap., 30th verse. No
doubt the writer intended the allegory to be understood or he would not have referred to the increase in
the length of the days after the winter solstice and
the decrease after the summer solstice.

The circle, with the cross inside, is the symbol of our Earth; it means body or trials.

Here are the symbols of the planets, in their order from the Sun ☉. Mercury ☿. Venus ♀. Earth ⊕. Moon ☽. Mars ♂. Jupiter ♃. Saturn ♄. Uranus ♅. Neptune ♆. Because of the rapidity of writing the uniformity and purity of the circle and its parts has not been kept as of old, either in the symbols of signs or planets, yet the novice can trace the intent.

. Here are the symbols of the signs of the Zodiac.

Aries -♈- a mental fire sign. Tauru -♉- an earth vital sign. Gemini -♊-·an air neantral sign. Cancer ·♋- is a mental water sign. Leo -♌- is a vital fire sign Virgo -♍- is a neutral earth sign. Libra -♎- is a mental air sign. Scorpio - ♏ - is a vital water sign. Sagittarius - ♐ - is a neutral fire sign. Capricornus - ♑ - is a mental earth sign. Aquarius - ♒ - is a vital air sign. Pisces - ♓ - is a neutral water sign.

The serpent, with his tail in his mouth is the symbol of the East India religion and stands for eternal life. Since time unknown, the circle has been the symbol of the sun, the life giver. Nothing can live without the sun.

The half circle or crescent is the symbol of the Turkish, or Mohammedan religion, which is the religion of a third part of the people of the globe. It means, to them, spirit and they claim there is no happiness outside of the spirit state.

Since time immemoral the half circle has been the symbol of the Moon.

If as before stated, the three symbols, the circle, half circle, and the cross, possess symbolic meaning, it must go farther and affect man, in some way in accordance with those symbols, (. e.) the circle, half circle and cross.

The circle stands for eternal life. Then we must have lived before, for a thing that has a beginning must have an ending, if so this life can only be one station or scene in the great drama of life.

The half circle stands for spirit, a transient position.

The cross represents the load, or burden, obstacle or hindrance from progress between the transient state of life. The cross in the circle refers to this particular earth life, as we could not know anything without experience, whatever we might have known in a former life or plan would have no influence on this earth life, that undoubtedly was what the writer intended to convey by the story of the temptation in the garden of Eden, or the eating of the tree of knowledge of good and evil. It is not until we compare these stories with astrology that they become rational.

The symbol of Mercury is made up of the three great symbols. The circle, the half circle and the cross. The symbols denote the direction or kind of influence the planet has upon man, and this is mani-. fest in accordance with the position and strength of the planet, or its relative position to other planets.

Though some of the planets are called good and some evil, they are all good or evil according to the influence they exert from their position. Though Mars is a very evil planet, without his influence we would have no force or energy, though if evily aspected, he causes us to use that force for bad purposes. Mercury possessing all of the symbols (i. e.) all of the attributes, acts good if in conjunction with good planets and evil if with evil planets.

Wherever the cross is found uppermost the evil predominates, so Mercury increases the good influence of Venus or Jupiter, because the cross is all below, and it increases the evil of Mars or Saturn.

If alone, not evily aspected, its influence increases mentality and spirituality, and if favorably 'nfluenced by Jupiter, the native will make money through those mental talents, as directed by Mercury's position and aspects, where his influence predominates. If evily aspected he will make a sharp trickster and hypocrite in the direction his influence leads.

The ancients understood this, and that is why all births were formerly registered in the nearest church to the locality of birth.

The cross above the circle is most evil and below the least, thus the half circle or spirituality is above, in Mercury, and the cross below, but with Mars, the cross is above.

When a man's energies and vitality is strong, he is apt to go to extremes in the direction his morals lead, a knave or a religious tyrant.

Venus is symbolized with the circle and the cross beneath. She is called the Goddess of love and beauty. If well placed and aspected, she produces saintly people, if evily stationed and aspected, she produces, leud, bad-principled people.

Mars is the first planet outside our earth and the cross stands above the circle, he is the God of War, and is bringing good or evil effects all the time, as he daily changes his position. He causes impulsive murders, and when evily aspected to Mercury, he produces tricksters and thieves, who would not hesitate at murder. His cross above the circle, is what gave rise to the story of the Christ or spirituality being crucified upon the cross, as the circle or Sun's influence is only partially felt upon our earth, and without the Sun's influence nothing can live.

Mars, the God of War, when evily aspected to spiritual planets, has caused the religious wars that have shaken our poor old mother earth to its foundation.

Jupiter is the God of Wealth and his symbol is made up of the cross and the half circle on the same level. Thus showing the rich man holds his wealth on a level or above his spirituality. Thus it is easier for the camel to pass the needle's eye than for a

rich man to enter the kingdom of heaven. Yet all
things are possible with God." Thus Jupiter may be
so aspected that he is a blessing or a curse to the
world.

Saturn is symbolized by the cross and two half
circles, forming the letter S backward to the cross,
showing he may be very evil or very spiritual, though
his spirituality is apt to be manifest in a concealed
manner, and his evil in long drawn out influence,
but all for man's ultimate good.

Uranus, the son of the Sun God, about to rule for
a thousand years, tears down to build up better. His
symbol is the circle, the two half circles and the
cross, sometimes made up like Mars with a dot in
the circle, showing he has or will have, great power
during the next thousand years, as he rules spirituality for that time, and under his rule man is to be
judged, or judge himself, as he strives to overcome
self. Uranus will help him.

Uranus and Neptune are of the higher octave, and
their influence was not felt for 26,000 years, until
about two thousand years ago or Christ's time.
Though not supposed to be discovered until March
13th, 1781, his existence was known to ancient astrologers, and as he took the place of rule of our
earth about sixty years ago, when the sun, in the
great Zodiac is supposed to have entered Aquarius,
after Uranus left the sign last.

Uranus enters the sign Aquarius again in 1912 and
reigns with his father, the Sun, for a thousand years.
His coming was "As a thief in the night," no one
knows just when his rule begins, hence the wise virgins will have their lamps trimmed and filled, but
the slack and delinquent will be rushing to the astrologers to know what is coming next, and how to
shape their course, and a clear conscience will be a
good thing to have about you as well as astrological
knowledge.

Uranus especially rules Spain, the dying relic of
the Papal power, which Uranus is tearing down to
build better.

The Papal power has ever made much of the

cross (i. e.) been ruled by the cross. She is ruled by the sign Sagittarius, whose symbol is the double cross.

Uranus was in that sign when Spain lost her Armada, when she lost her colonies, and again in 1898 when she lost the balance of her colonies, and since that Spain has made great progress, but in doing so she has been compelled to cut down the power of the Papal church.

The United States is ruled jointly by Gemini, the sign opposite to Sagittarius, and whose symbol is the broken stem of the cross, as Gemini rules North America. But the Declaration of Independence came in July, so Cancer is the direct ruler of the United States, the symbol of the two circles and two half circles. This is a commercial water sign. So you may see the reason the United States is rapidly becoming the commercial master of the world and her naval power has never been defeated and is the real ruler of the wave.

Neptune is symbolized by four crosses and a half circle. Three of the crosses are above the half circle and one below.

Remember Mythology makes Neptune ruler of sea and land and of earthquakes, and as mythology, like the Bible, is the concealed writings of astrologers.

Neptune is the internal disturber, he is also the John the Baptist born six months before the Savior. Look where Neptune is to-day in Cancer, nearing the great war sign Leo, a vital sign, and Uranus, six signs opposite nearing the vital sign Aquarius, where he begins his rule.

This is in the top of the celestial head or spirituality, where man will learn that justice to one another is the only road to happiness. But before this can take place all old things must pass away and all thnigs become new." See chapter on the "New Jerusalem." So Neptune is doing his work of internal disturbances. Look at the earthquakes, disappearing and rising islands, and terrific volcanic action, and as this must increase, social unrest will also increase, and old systems will be swept away and the new systems, whatever they may be will be brought in their stead.

Now let us show the part the United States was destined to play in the great drama. It was all pictured in symbols by the old astrologers who wrote the books of the Bible, and under the astrologers interpretation, the Bible stories become reasonable and pretty, and the lovers of our country and our flag should be prouder than ever, and more watchful and determined that overt acts in any direction, whether of rich or poor, bond or free, religious or non religious shall not destroy our power and usefulness

Let us here note 12 is a prophetic number, see farther on the allegory of the prodigal son.

Remember there were twelve sons of Ishmael—representing twelve princes or twelve cities.

Let me here state, the starry constellations were once one and the same as the twelve signs of the Zodiac, but have moved thirty degrees west of the signs, thus become the Ishmael or illegal child of Abram, or God given influence to the signs of the Zodiac, which receive their influence from greater constellation influence farther away.

In the 49th chapter of Genesis, Jacob is supposed to be blessing his twelve sons, but in reality is giving the influence of the twelve signs of the Zodiac.

In astrology the signs of the Zodiac are the basic principle, and the writers of the Bible were not teaching astrology but were prophesying by astrology of future events.

I wish it distinctly understood here, that any astrologer will develope clairvoyant powers, as did Daniel, and the best astrologers combine clairvoyancy with their work, this is why the Christ is so often foretelling the future by clairvoyancy, and this stamps everything as eminating from a universal intelligence and a universal plan.

The twelve epostles of the Son of God, or the Sun God are the twelve signs of the Zodiac.

Now notice in Revelations XII-1 "And there appeared a great wonder in heaven; a woman clothed with the Sun, and the Moon under her feet, and upon her head a crown of twelve stars: And she being with child cried, travailing in birth, and pained to be delivered."

Remember the church is symbolized by a woman, as Christ speaks of his bride, but no particular church, for he says, "where two or three are gathered together in my name there am I in the midst there of."

The woman to be delivered was the religious denominations who were crying for a government where they could worship according to the dictates of their conscience. Daniel symbolizes the nations as beasts of prey, devouring by conquest. The United States is the man child, the first to grant religious freedom.

The woman, or people of the reform churches, were given two great wings, (the fore and aft sails of that time) with which she fled to the wilderness where she is to be fed, (spiritually) for times, time and a half a time— 1260 years, or to about the year 2910, when a universal change will take place. This bars no church or creed.

Like the Sons of Ishmael representing twelve cities these twelve stars on the woman's head represent the twelve colonies which first established this country.

These were religious colonies, one of them, Baltimore, Maryland, was Catholic, but had left the church for broader views, but became the Judas Iscariot, and went back to the mother church who demands allegience, before that to any monarch. This is not aimed at the Catholic church, or any other.

The woman clothed with the Sun, means England, the strongest nation which claimed all of the colonies.

The Moon under the woman's feet was France, the next strongest nation, which supported the woman, or religious colonies when the man child was born.

Those who would ask "What about the thirteen colonies?" should remember there were but twelve

at first and but twelve signers of the Declaration of
Independence, one a Catholic. Canada was strongly
Catholic, but did not come into the union, and
neither did Georgia until after the war began.

The colonies were very religious, but we must remember there were some strong free thinkers, like
Thomas Paine, Benjamin Franklin and Thomas Jefferson, whose motto was "Eternal vigilance is the
price of liberty." Thus religious liberty like human
justice depends upon eternal vigilance.

Here is a strange coincidence.

The serpent in the garden of Eden denied God's
rule, yet he was a wise vigilant being.

The first flag of our country was made up of stripes
and the picture of a rattle snake with the words,
"Don't tread on me."

The rattle snake has no eyelids, he is vigilant, and
he never strikes without warning. It has been suggested that a free thinker like the gentleman mentioned above, have risen so far above the influence
of the stars as to be more near the master of their
own destiny, and such men are generally rigidly
just.

The first real American flag or stars and stripes,
flung to the breeze by the immortal Paul Jones had
but twelve stars, and the colonies at first demanded
but twelve stars to represent the twelve apostles, the
additional stars represent the additional states as
they came into the union. The blue field represents
the blue canopy of heaven that extends over all
alike, the stars—the stars of heaven that shine for
all alike, the stripes—the stripes the vigilant must
expect, who are ready to sacrifice self for the principles, the most beautiful emblem God's Sun ever
shone on, stand for. The red stripes represent red
blood that flows in all men's veins alike giving all an
equal right before the law.

The white stripes represent that purity of purpose
every man should aim for. Thus every soul should
jealously watch and care for our flag and the principles it stands for "the right to life, liberty and the
pursuit of happiness." Equality before the law, free-

dom of thought. Free speech, and a free press. Such rights and privileges wrong no man.

He wro tries to rule other men's reason by law and by force, is a dangerous man to the liberties and rights of his fellow man, and should be watched and pointed out to all other men as dangerous to the welfare of the community.

Our Christian friends will often say, "I will not accept anything outside of the Bible." Very well, here is a quotation from Gallatians, 4th and 24th, speaking of Abraham, it says:

"Which things are an allegory; for these are the two covenants."

If the story of Abraham is an allegory then the story of the Son of God is an allegory also, for the Bible itself does not speak positive on the matter, but says, "And Jesus himself began to be about thirty years of age, being (as was supposed) the son of Joseph." Luke 3 and 23d. As there is not a scrap of evidence to be found, which was written prior to 150 years after the, supposed, birth of Christ, it is plain they could not write with much certainty; they then make the sad mistake of giving one man two fathers, as is done in writing up the genealogy. Matthew 1st chap., and Luke 3d chap. As these two chapters disagree, such genealogy would not stand in our courts; then why should any one else accept it? If we found a book in our public schools containing so many inconsistencies and contradictions, as my Agnostic's Lament, points out in the Bible, it would be quickly kicked out.

Volumes of testimony might be written in proof that the whole Bible is but a succession of stories of astrology in allegory. It is admitted by prominent theologians that the four gospels were not written by the apostles; how could they be? If Abraham and his progeny are an allegory then of course Christ and his disciples are allegorical characters. Many will say, "Have we not got the Jews and the Jewish history as evidence? I answer yes, but Jewish history is very lame, besides they denied there ever was such a being as Christ.

Let us now consider the ZODIAC IN CONNEC-
TION WITH A BRIEF HISTORY OF ALL RELI-
GION.

As the Sun passes from sign to sign, through the
great Zodiac, it seems to change all nature, on our
Earth, even to man's religion. Thus the Zodiac, understood, will give us the rise and fall of the various
forms of worship; though it must be remembered
fragments, of a long lost form of worship, will crop
out under favoring planetary influences, and when the
Sun transits opposite signs or the signs giving them
birth. Just as Mormonism is a relic of sex worship.

That we may best understand this let us take the
49th chapter of Genesis, and we will find that Jacob,
when blessing his twelve sons, was really giving the
influences and attributes of the 12 signs of the Zodiac.
But, to do this, we must at the same time give the
foundation of all religion, which seems to be expressed in the movements of the heavenly bodies.

The old astrologers were, no doubt, much farther
advanced in the science of astrology than our present
astronomers or astrologers, and they knew of the
influence of the heavenly bodies, and that civilization
would go backward, and so they left records, on the
pyramids, in the Bible and many other enduring
places.

The Nebular theory holds that all of the Sun's satellites were once a part of the Sun and were thrown
off from it.

Thinking people are beginning to recognize that
thoughts are things and that the difference between
mind and matter is, simply, that what we call mind
is that thought on a higher plane of vibration, acting
on that thought on a lower plane of vibration, which
we call matter. The meaning of all this is that the
Sun is our proper home, or the true Garden of Eden,
from which we were cast out, and we cannot get back
until we conquer all selfish and foolish desires, and
the Sun is the flaming sword, turning every way,
which the Bible speaks of.

While the Sun in the great Zodiac changes its influence upon us, every two thousand years, we are

born to live and die at least once during the period the Sun is transiting each sign of the Zodiac, and at every round, those who are fit will go to a higher sphere, and those who are not must remain for another 26,000 years, before they get another opportunity to graduate.

The final graduation takes place just before the Sun leaves Capricornus and enters the firey Sagittarius.

## ORIGIN OF EASTER FESTIVAL.

The celebration of the Easter festival dates so far back beyond the Christian era that its origin is shadowed in mystery. The proper date for the celebration has been a bone of contention among church people of all ages.

The reason it has been a matter of such extensive controversy is the uncertainty for the establishing of the New Year's day or birth of the Sun.

Almost any encyclopedia will tell you that Easter was celebrated long ages before the Christian era.

Zell's encyclopedia says: "This term has been variously derived—some taking it from the Saxon Oster" —to rise, and others from the name of a heathen goddess, Eastre or Ostra, whose rites the Saxons were accustomed to celebrate at this time of the year and on account of which the month of April was styled Eastermonth, in their calendar.

All authority admits that the celebration of Easter, supposed to celebrate the resurrection of Christ, is also the same day observed in honor of Cyble, the mother of the Babylonian deity. Thus we have the evidence that the custom is much older than the Christian era.

Now let us prove that it was originated in honor of the new born Sun. But, here we are somewhat at bay to defend our own position, and why?. The answer is that man's calculations for the beginning of the new year were not very accurate, and so his year varied in length and some nations fixed the birth of the Sun on the day in which the days begin to lengthen, or Dec. 25, when we celebrate Christ's birthday, the Son or Sun manifest in the flesh. Others celebrated the 21st of March as the New Year, as this was when the Sun reigned in full glory over his enemies. These two dates alone should be evidence enough to establish beyond a shadow of a doubt that the whole religious scheme is based upon astronomical periods.

Now let us give religious testimony. I will quote from Potter's Bible encyclopedia: "In the most ancient worship the seventh day of 'Passion week,' the 'Great Sabbath,' was osberved as a day of strict fasting, watch was kept during the night until cock crow, the time our Lord was believed to have risen, when the exclamation of the worshipers burst forth: "The Lord is risen! the Lord is risen! The Lord is risen indeed!"

This exclamation shows they calculated the day from 12 o'clock at night, and the Sun would then be just entering the sign Virgo, the sign of the virgin, or 6th house, thus he is born of the sign of the virgin, she being the mother of the God of day.

Now quoting from Potter again, "The Lord is risen indeed," that is to say, it is manifest in daylight, as that was announced by the crowing of the cock. "Then followed a day of rejoicing. The Lord's supper was observed. New church converts were baptized, prisoners and slaves were set free, business was suspended in the courts of law, and the week was devoted to enjoyment."

Even this religious authority admits that the custom is of much earlier origin than the Christian era. Again quoting from Potter—"This word is from Saxon origin, from a Goddess "Estera," who was honored, in the spring time, about the season of the passover. The festival of the resurrection of Christ coming at the same time, the name became associated with it."

Farther on in "Bible Astrology" I have shown where not only the religious forms split and quarreled with the people, but among themselves, and even split Astrological forms. One part as above

stated holding the birth of the Sun was at the 21st
of March. This was in accordance with the Helio
Centric system, and figuring the day to be born at
midnight, the Sun would be passing through the sign
Virgo. Now by quoting from page 28 of my "Periodicity" you will notice there was still a dispute in the
matter and that was settled by Julius Caesar, by the
assistance of Chaldeic mathematicians, who fixed
the birth of the Sun or winter solstice to take place
Dec. 25th at 30 minutes past one in the morning;
that gave the Sun time to leave the sign Virgo,
thus be born of theVirgin, and by sunrise to be at
the 1st degree of Aries Helio Centricly, that is, the
divisions of the earth corresponding with the signs
of the Zodiac, will in any form you put it make the
Sun born of the Virgin, thus if you count Dec. 25th
as the birth of the Sun, at 1:30 the Sun will be passing out of that division of the earth corresponding
with Virgo, and if at sunrise, the divisions Virgo will
cover the 1st degree of Capricornus the goat. So it
does not matter which system you use, Helio or Geo,
in either case by that arrangement the Sun is born
of the Virgin.

Again, Dec. 25, at midnight, when the day is born,
or the Sun of God is born, the sign Virgo, the virgin,
is on the ascendant. So much testimony must prove
one of two things, either the story is based on Astrology or Astrology is a proof of the truth of the
birth and existence of Christ, the Son of the Sun God.

This can be more readily seen by the use of my
Solar Bioscope or a map of the Zodiac containing the
degrees, months and days, and a smaller map, representing the earth, revolving on its axis, inside the
larger map, when holding the sign Aries at the left
hand, Capricornus at top.

Undoubtedly this question was old, even at the
time of Julius Caesar.

Religion was the politics of the ancients, and in
fact was the bone of contention and war, over the
greater portion of the earth down to almost the present time, but at the beginning of the Christian era
there was undoubtedly a strong attempt to harmon-

ize the two factions and make the two systems agree
so Dec. 25th was generally settled upon as the proper
time as birth of the Sun, but there was yet three
months of cold dreary winter, so added to the story.
The savior lies in the grave or descends into hades
for three days and then in April they celebrate his
resurrection. Thus every phase of the allegorical
story is accounted for.

If there is no connection between the Astrological
phenomena, of the Sun's birth, December 25, or of
the 21st of March, making the Sun born of the Virgin
Sign, Virgo, how is it that it also agrees with the
custom of one of our churches who celebrate the 8th
of December as the day of immaculate conception,
which would bring the birth of Christ in September,
the Sign of the Virgin. This should convince Christians that either the whole religious scheme is based
upon Astronomical positions or testified to by those
positions. I leave it for you to judge.

Of course I know, longitude and latitude will be
brought forward as well as discrepancies in calendar
dates will be brought forward as arguments against
this theory, but I challenge the world to disprove this
testimony.

There is much more evidence of the same nature
that can be piled up which proves that though the
root of the word—Easter—may have been Saxon, the
custom was practiced before there was a Saxon people, and that it originated with Sun worship.

Those who have read the earlier editions of my
Bible Astrology will remember how the story of the
Son of God and the story of the Sun God are one and
the same thing. Now let us note the desire to re-
duce this story to the comprehension of the weaker
intellects of man and we will find it testified to by
20 crucified saviors as follows:

We find several passages in the Bible that speak
of story writers. Thus this religious matter was
written up in story, in other words in allegory, now
let us bring testimony, right from the Bible. For
this, look to Galatians IV—22 to 26. The 24th verse
reads "which things are an allegory." Now if Abra-

ham and his two sons were an allegory, and Christ was of the seed of Abraham, the whole story would seem to be an allegory.

Now let us not quarrel over the matter, whether or not there was a man in the flesh called Christ or whether a being we recognize of that name was born of immaculate conception or not, or whether it was only an allegorical story. The ideal character is the highest type of perfection man can conceive of, and as thoughts are things these must spring from a supreme origin, and his wisdom is recorded in the books of nature, to be read by astrologers, who were formerly called wise men. These were the ordained priests as nature especially fits them for such work, therefore the church people of today are turning away from their only defence when they turn against the astrologer, and the astrologer and reformers and followers in any new thought idea are turning against their strongest friend and bullwark when they turn against the Christ idea, so let us not dispute whether it be Chrishna, Benpander, Jesus of Nazareth, Buddah, or any one of the other mentioned crucified saviors. If we speak of the Christ we have in heart the ideal and the universe is filled with the Christ idea ready to come to our assistance in accordance with the strength of faith, manifest in our deeds and earnest supplications, yet that need not deter us from seeking truth.

In some of the spring time festivals called Easter, the date was fixed at April 14th, others April 16th. But the Jews who were really Sun worshipers, began their year with the first new moon in March and to celebrate their passover with the first full moon after the 21st of March. This, of course, had to make a movable festival, and caused dissentions and an endless controversy. It is none of our business what church people do, if we believe the old Astrologers who wrote the Bible, knew their business. The churches must soon give up the ghost, for it says of "The Mother of harlots I will make a bed for her and her children I will kill with death."

In another place it says "Come out of them, Oh! my people." So it matters not whether they change their Easter or not. Unless they change their conduct and become real followers of Christ who had no place to lay his head, and become the friends of the common people as Christ was represented to do, the churches will have no followers, but the stars (of the social) heavens will fall to the earth like a tree casting its untimely fruit shaken by a mighty wind."

This great unrest marks the beginning of the end of the Pisces world, and a new heavens and a new earth will take its place (i. e.) the Aquarius world, and happy indeed will be the lot of those who live when graft and the lust for wealth and cheaply bought fame will give way to common sense and honesty. (See chapter on New Jerusalem.)

It is easy for the astrologer to see where man's tampering with the truth gleaned from God's Books of Nature is at fault.

### GOD'S GOOD BOOKS.

When we compare, the little we know of Mother Earth to what we do not know of her, and then compare that to our attempts to fathom the depths of space, we should be able to see the individual man cannot amount to so much to God, in comparison as a honey bee does to man.

Now imagine the honey bee declaring man made, not only the bees' hive, but all of the structures of man and nature, for the bee's particular benefit, and then, inspires the bee to build his especial work, and possibly write a book of instructions for his guidance. It would be about as reasonable as man has been in his declaration that the great intelligent Creator stooped so low as to write, or cause to be written a book so full of mistakes as our Bible, and then leave it to blundering man to translate and interpret, when He must have known that men in their prejudices and weakness would do what they have done—butcher and persecute each other for hundreds of years, for God's sake.

Is it not natural that a great and allwise being would write his book in nature's works, which are more enduring than the material, language and customs of man?

Not only the Bible, but all of the histories of man and works of art of man show conclusively that all religion is based upon natural law, and Astronomy or Astrology is "The stone cut out without hands, which must again become the chief corner stone of the structure.

When one notices the apparent endeavors of religious people to use the church and religion to hold the people in subjection while being robbed by the privileged class, while throwing every obstacle possible in the way of honest research and progress, it makes one look with suspicion upon all forms of religion.

In the original text of Genesis, 1-14, my books of reference say it reads: "Let there be light, to divide the day from the night, and let them be for SIGNS, and for SEASONS, and for NATIONS."

The last six words have been left out.

I will now proceed to show that the Bible is Astrology in allegory and that all religion is based upon Astrology.

All history shows the Jews were Sun worshipers, and Jews have told me their old prayer books contained a picture of the Zodiac. See what John says:

John 1, 1: "In the beginning was the word, and the word was with God.".

Now, what was the word?

Potter's Bible Encyclopedia says: "LOGOS, the word, a title given to our Lord and Savior, so designated not only because the Father first created and still governs all things, by him, but because, as men discover their sentiments and designs to one another by the intervention of words, speech or discourse, so God by his SON or SUN discovers his gracious designs to men."

Now then, the question arises, as nothing could grow or exist without the warming influence of the Sun, we must ask ourselves was the SUN meant, by "the word?" And was the Son in the flesh, an allegory, or was the word also manifest in the flesh?

Among the many Bibles, all of which are supposed to be, by the supporters, to be right from the hand of God, the oldest is supposed to be the Hindoo Vedas, which affirms the independence of spirit from matter, though Herodatus claims the Egyptians were the first who taught the immortality of the soul, of man.

The Aryan name of God was "Div.," which is said to stand for the clear light of day, and this word has become the root word of all Gods of worship, though somewhat changed until it has come down to us as Deity.

It is said by scholars that the Hindoo Scriptures teem with praises to light and heat, which are termed the workers of miracles by the Sun God or starry robed ruler, Lord.

The Hebrew is the sacred or secret language of the ancient priesthood, and the word is pronounced Yod—or Adonis—the Sun, or He; Vau; He; said to be pronounced but once a year, by the high priest.

The Nebula theory supposes the Sun gave birth to each one of its satellites being torn from its side; thus Mother Earth is Eve torn from the side of Adam, or a rib of Adam. Adonis, the Sun, just as the Moon is supposed to have been torn from the side of Mother Eve (Earth).

Each one of the Sun's satellites are counted among the subordinate or lesser Gods, each ruling a day of the week.

The Sun—Michael—rules Sunday.

The Moon—Gabriel—rules Monday.

Mars—Samael—rules Tuesday.

Mercury—Raphael—rules Wednesday.

Jupiter—Sachiel—rules Thursday.

Venus—Anael—rules Friday.

Saturn—Cassiel—rules Saturday.

All of the planets bear more than one name, and the Moon has many names; thus the Gods and Goddesses of Mythology are continually referred to in literature; but known to but few. The following are a few of the names of these Gods, which are of the planets, though sometimes confused as they became known by more than one name.

Sun—God of light Apollon Gerek—Apollo Roman—God of music, poetry and male beauty.

Moon—Queen of the night. Diana Roman Goddess of hunting—Minerva daughter of Jupiter, sometimes confounded with the Queen of Hades.

Vulcan—Pluto, God of the infernal regions, a physician and blacksmith.

Nearest satellite to the Sun.

Mercury—second satellite from the Sun and messenger of the Gods, called the Son of Jupiter and God of trade and eloquence.

Venus, third child of the Sun. Goddess of beauty—Aphrodite Goddess of passion, and other names.

Earth—fourth from the Sun, called Reah, wife of Uranus, the Son of the Sun God, a great spiritual planet, the children of Uranus and Earth are the spirits of men receiving their lessons under the care of Mother Earth, who is fitting them through hard experience for an independent life in the spirit state.

Earth is also called Zenda—thought by some to be the prison of the souls of men, who are held here in durance until freed by death, for eating of the forbidden fruit (i. e., taking wives from the daughters of men they saw that they were fair; and they took themselves wives of all which they chose."

Emerson says: "This Earth is an abiding place for God's insane angles."

Aries is the constellation, once at the head of the Zodiac and called the God of War and the home of Mars—the God of War, the fifth planet from the Sun.

The Asteroids is a group of small stars between Mars and Jupiter, over a hundred, supposed to be a planet or satellite of the Sun, broken up; it furnished a number of Gods, of mythology.

Jupiter is the 7th of the Sun's children, called Jove, or God of Thunder, or Zeus, God of Gods, because of his great size. Also God of Wealth.

Saturn—in Astrology called the 7th body, in reality the 8th thrown from the Sun, is called Chronos, the God of Agriculture.

Uranus, the 9th from the Sun, the Son of the Sun God and husband of Reah, the Earth.

Neptune numbered as 10th planet from the Sun, and is called the God of the Waves and the God of the Earthquakes.

Volumes could be written in proof that all of man's Bibles and his Gods are taken from Astronomy or formally called Astrology.

As every one of our solar satellites have been called Gods and the Sun worshipped as the God of Gods, and as it certainly is the ruler of all life, nothing could live without its heat, light and magnetic power, how perfectly natural that mankind, who is so prone to worship what they do not understand should become Sun worshipers. It would be just as natural for deeper students to point to the fact that there must be powers beyond the Sun, and so our Sun becomes the instrument in the hands of the universal ruler; then as to the Sun seems to die, be crucified between November and December, every year, and is reborn on the 25th day of December (i. e.) days begin to lengthen. He is the Sun of God, who is crucified on the cross formed by the summer and winter solstice and the spring and fall, equinox, see chapter on New Testament.

)That this story might be more comprehensive to the common people, it is woven into fiction in every language, and so we have 20 crucified saviors. Nineteen of these died on the cross hundreds of years before Christ. These come in their order as follows:

No.
1. Thulis of Egypt—1700 B. C.
2. Chrishna of Hindoo—1200 B. C.
3. Crite of Chaldea—1200 B. C.
4. Mithra of Persia—1200 B. C.
5. Hesus of the Celtice Drodes—834 B. C.
6. Thammuz of Syria—800 B. C.
7. Indra of Thibet—725 B. C.
8. Bali of Crissa—725 B. C.
9. Ivo of Nepaul—620 B. C.
10. Sakiah Budah, India—600 B. C.
11. Aceston, of Greece—600 B. C.
12. Atys, of Pheygia—600 B. C.
13. Witoba, of the Telingonese—550 B. C.

14.  Prometheus, of Greece—547 B. C.
15   Quirinus, of Rome—400 B. C.
16.  Txion, of Rome—400 B. C.
17.  Quexalocote, of Mexico—327 B. C.
18.  Denatat, of Siam—300 B. C.
19.  Appolonius of Tyana in Capidone—300 B. C.
20.  Jesus of Nazareth, some say proper name Ben pandor.  The history of the religions of all ages, and of all of these crucified saviors recites the history of a Sun God, born of a Virgin, pursued by a great Dragon of the skies, and finally crucified and reborn on the 25th day of December, when the days begin to lengthen.

The following clipping was handed me by a reporter.  It is dated May 14, 1908:

In May, 1898, there met a congress of theological professors and profound thinkers who discussed "The influence of history upon theology and religion."

One of the most scholarly papers of the lot was presented by Prof. R. M. Wenley, Ph. D., Sc. D., of the University of Michigan, who said that one good of the historical critical method has been to make the Bible a familiar book again.  "Yet," said he, "its consequences count heavily on the negative side and bear hardly on natural piety.  It seems we know very little, in strict historical parlance, either of the author of the New Testament or of Jesus.  In short, the materials for a biography of Jesus do not exist.  Similarly, comparative religion has shown that christianity adopted elements, from other faiths, or at least developed along parallel lines.  My own conviction is that this negative process is destined to travel even farther, probably during the life time of many among us.  And it may very well be that, when criticisms come to clarify its evidence, and to reconstruct the situation from an exact historical standpoint, we shall stand aghast stricken and helpless."

Any person who pursues the history of the matter will find volumes of evidence to prove the Astronomical scheme is the basis of all religion.  It is the stone cut out without hands that must again become the chief stone of the corner of the structure.

Here is an admission that there is no material for the Biography of Jesus."

Other theologians have admitted there cannot be found a word concerning the life of Christ that was written until a hundred and fifty years after Christ.

While Atheism, or the denying the existence of a supreme being, or a future life, in the face of fact and reason, is foolish, but no more so than is declared faith of the various religious followers who declare you must have faith, and if you dare to give up your faith in our church you are doomed to everlasting torment.

To be converted to Parsisms, Buddhism, Mohammedanism, Mormonism, Spiritualism or Christianity you must have faith; aye, give up all reason and accept the doctrine, or be damned, and if you accept the wrong one you will be damned by all of the rest; so you are damned if you do, and you are damned if you don't.

The necessity for faith is pointed out by all believers in any religion and Christians call attention to Mark VII., 2:6, "When Jesus made his second visit to Nazareth," he laid his hand upon a few sick folk and healed them, "but could there do no mighty work," because of unbelief.

Now we must remember the very last thing when Christ was on the cross he lost his faith and cried out, "My God, my God, why hast thou forsaken me?"

Now it seems to me when a man gives up his reason and accepts the teachings of any men, who has no means of knowing any more about a matter than he, is no longer a man but a puppet to be buffeted around by any one who chances to have a stronger mind and hypnotizing power greater than his own. God has printed his laws in the heart of every man, to know right from wrong, according to the power and light within him.

We know that men become selfish and will "steal the livery of heaven to serve the devil." Therefore God's religion will be manifest in man's desire to serve God by doing right, but when a man pretends that his faith in God will insure him a pearly seat at

the right hand of God, at the same time gives him a
license to continually wrong his fellow-man, and this
in the face of the fact; that Christ is said to have
had no place to lay his head and was forever making
war on wealth gatherers. This very fact is the
strongest argument in favor of the divinity of the
Christ principle. This should settle it in the mind of
every man, whether the ideal character of Christ, is
merely an allegory of the Sun, or whether he represented the word (i. e.) the Sun, in the flesh, or
whether he was born of an immaculate conception, it
matters not.

Thoughts are things; and God, the eternal principal, is the author of all things, and as millions of
people for many years have believed in and preached
the ideal character and love of Christ until a mighty
sea of that thought principle surrounds us and leads
the way to a higher plane of being. So let us stick
to the ideal character, and if we do that we must love
the truth, and if we love truth honest investigation
is our God-given right, and woe to him who attempts
to lead us from it or throws stumbling blocks in our
way, for the Divine principle of truth will remain
with us and defend us.

The Progressive Thinker, of the date of April 23rd,
1910, says: "A German scientist has been producing
so much evidence to prove there never was such a
being as Christ. The Emperor has become so interested that he has had the preachers closeted with
him in hot discussion which lasted into the wee hours
of the night." It also states that when the question
was asked, of Rabbi Hirsch of Chicago, "Was Jesus
ever on earth, material?" he replied, "Any person
who attempts to prove that he was will have a hard
task."

"But," asked his questioner, "would it not be natural for the Jews to deny that he ever did exist?"

The Rabbi replied, "The Jewish people would naturally be proud of such an honor, that a son of God
should be born of their race."

It has always been the Christian's boast that the
Bible has stood the test of criticism, and nothing
could shake it.

It is truly a great book and I do not wish to detract one iota from its real value or hinder its usefulness. But, you surround any book with a halo of
sacredness and then condemn, ostracize and possibly
murder every person who dares to adversely criticise
its pages, and it, too, will stand the test of ages.

Go back into the pages of history, and read how
every religious reform has had to fight its way, not
only by argument, but with carnal weapons until riv-
ers of blood flowed from innocent people for opinion's sake, and you will no longer wonder why the
Bible has stood the test of ages, notwithstanding
its glaring errors and inconsistencies, but you will
wonder why we have made as much progress as
we have.

The thunder of the preachers, from the pulpits of
the followers of Martin Luther, were answered by the
thunder from the vatican, and then from the throats
of artillery. Indeed, the hardships of our forefathers
who came to the wilderness and fought for religious
liberty, should have taught them justice, instead,
they became the traducers of the fair name of the
great and good Thomas Paine, who is credited with
having written the Declaration of Independence, if
he did not write the Constitution of the United States,
yet any person who reads his works without prejudice must admit he is fair and unbiased, yet his books
have been prohibited in some of the public libraries,
and may be yet for what I know.

Is it any wonder the Bible or any books surrounded
with such conditions will stand the test of age? Even
so short a time as two years ago, attempts were made
to suppress, by law, religious liberties of astrologers
and spiritual mediums, and have in some places surrounded them with so many restrictions as to make
their work impossible in that locality. It would not
be wise for them to claim that it is in the interest
of honesty, in the face of court records of some
preachers and church followers, number for number.

## PARALELLS OF THE OLD TESTAMENT.—PAS-

### SAGES AND TRUTHS IN ASTROLOGY.

In studying these lessons we should put away all partiality and prejudice, and seek only the truth.

One should look up the Bible passages for himself, and neither let the author or a bigoted Bible student interpret them for himself.

Before proceeding you should become familiar with the chart of the Zodiac and look at it frequently, at least every time it is announced the sun has passed over into another sign.

A brief outline of the Old Testament runs that: "In the beginning God created the earth." It does not say when the beginning was, or what God made the earth out of.

The writer is simply trying to make comprehensive, a work too vast to incompass in one small book the size of the Bible, therefore he leaves much to the reader's judgment.

What did God create the earth out of?

If God is omnipresent and omnipotent, there can be no place, not even an atom, where he is not. Therefore there is nothing but God, consequently mind and matter are one and the same thing.

Wise men are beginning to recognize that thoughts are things because we never created a thought, as we all have thoughts we do not want and have to fight them away and study hard to let in those thoughts we do want.

If everything is God, there can be no room for anything else but God. Then God had to create the earth out of himself.

If everything is thought, everything is life, and these living entities are continually trying to organize thoughts beneath them into Kingdoms of their own. This would imply that what we call matter is that mind on a lower plain of action than our own souls.

If God is everywhere, there is nothing but God, then God must have made all things out of himself, and there is no room for a devil, as the Bible says: "A house divided against itself can't stand."

If there is no devil what is evil?

It is plain, evil is unfinished good, or the greatest evil is to go back to a wrong, we have arisen above, just because we like it.

Would God build an everlasting hell for himself?

Man has reached a point of intelligence in which he is able to shape the course of animal life below him.

The cow or sheep whose life we take can no more comprehend man, than man can comprehend the ways of God or the unseen angles or spirits above us.

If a man is evolved, there must be a God, because if he did not always exist we have had eternity of the past to evolve a God, to rule over us, as well as we were evolved to rule over those below us. This gave rise to the idea that kings have a divine right to rule.

All nature teaches us evolution is a truth, because the wise can see the evidence before us every day.

We find evidence of evolution in the mechanical works of man. In his dress, in his own body, and in the bodies of the lower animals.

The buttoned shoe has given way to the elastic, but we often find buttons remaining. The necktie is the remnant of a great muffler our forefathers wore and called a stock. The buttons on the back of a frock coat were placed there to keep the sword belt up, to make it look trim and neat. The sword is gone, the belt is gone, but the buttons remains, as much as to say here is a relic of evolution.

The horse has the splints in his hoof, which goes to show he was once a five-toed animal. Man has muscles behind the ears. He once used to waggle the ears to drive the flies off, when he ran on all fours. He has no use for them now.

There are many organs in the human body that testify to the fact that man is an evolved being.

The coxigeous is the remains of a tail.

The appendix, which causes appendicities with no end of trouble and pain, is a useless organ. No physician can tell what purpose it once served.

The spleen is another organ that puzzles the scientists to discover its purpose, and there are many more evidences that man is an evolved being, but as all is God, man must be working along the lines of a great plan.

If the body of man is evolved and everything is mind, then it must be evident man lives again.

Yes, it holds good that man lives again. But does he hold to this identity? As nature is intelligence, and is so careful that nothing shall be lost. The destruction of an article leaves the same material to create another article. Nature will not let the most sacred thing of all, man's experience, be lost. Hence man must live again.

As man is an evolved being his experience must be necessarily from one life to another, consequently reincarnation must be a necessity.

God himself could not know the difference between pain and pleasure if he never thought of the two opposites. Therefore God must lay plans to get the experience.

Man could never know the difference between bitter and sweet if he never tasted of them.

Man comes to earth for experience, to build a spiritual kingdom larger that he may enjoy more because he knows more.

As man must educate the lower mind to build it into his kingdom he must come back to earth. Hence the spirit state is a period of rest. It is impossible to progress in the spirit state, man must come back to earth to progress. There is no material in the spirit state on which to build.

If there were a thousand of us, with palaces, grounds, libraries, art, music, games, everything the heart could wish, and we with nothing to do but enjoy ourselves, it would be our heaven, would it not? After we had enjoyed it over and over, it would finally become, so monotonous, it would become our hell.

Now we look across the street and see the people doing something over there, we would want to go over to see what they were doing, but it is slush, storm, hell between our once heaven and the new found place. But this outside hell is no worse than that place that has once been our heaven, so we plunge out and get on the other side to enjoy more because we know more.

Truly, evolution and reincarnation are necessities.

Is there any evidence that the Bible teaches reincarnation?

Yes, the Bible is full of it. II. Kings, 2d, 11th, says: "Elijah went up by a whirlwind of fire 880 years before Christ."

Malachi, 4-5, says: "Behold, I will send you Elijah the prophet before the coming of the great ard dreadful day of the Lord."

Matthew, 17 and 10-14, says: "And his disciples asked him, saying, Why then say the scribes that Elias (the Greek for Elijah) must first come? And Jesus answered and said unto them Elias truly shall first come, and restore all things. But I say unto you, That Elias is come ALREADY, and they know him not. Then the disciples understood that he spake unto them of John the Baptist."

Mark, 9-11, 13: "And they asked him, saying, Why say the scribes that Elias must first come? And he answered and told them, Elias, verily, cometh first. But I say unto you, That Elias is indeed come, and they have done unto him whatsoever they listed."

You know they took his head off.

Some who are prejudiced against reincarnation pretend to believe God meant to send John in the spirit of Elijah. What nonsense to lay God in a lie, when he said he would send Elijah and did not say he would send some other fellow in the spirit of Elijah.

Matthew XI-14: "And if ye will receive it, this is Elias, which was for to come."

St. John IX-1-2.: "And Jesus passed by; he saw a man which was blind from his birth.

2. And his disciples asked him, saying, Master, who did sin, this man or his parents, that he was born blind?"

Unless this man lived in a former life how could his sin cause him to be born blind?

Of course they understood and believed in reincarnation.

In this brief work I shall show that life on this earth is a school and that at certain periods there are graduation days and just as it would not be desirable to attempt to graduate a scholar who has just entered the school it is not desirable to graduate those who have not been reincarnated enough times to develop the proper character.

Matthew XIII-11 to 14. Shows it was destined some should not understand, and in Luke VIII-9, "And his disciples asked him, saying, What might this parable be?

10. "And he said, Unto you it is given to know the mysteries of the Kingdom of God: but to others in parables: that seeing they might not see, and hearing they might not understand."

If a man is not to understand how can he be blamed?

I will now show God's workshop or school room and explain some of the knotty Biblical passages.

God made the Earth in six days and rested on the seventh.

It is plain God did his work in weeks.

How long were these days and weeks?

God said to Adam, "The day thou eatest thereof thou shalt surely die."

Adam did not die for 600 years.

Did God lie or was he talking of a different kind of a day than man's twenty-four hour day?

Some try to explain he was talking of a spiritual death, but it requires a long stretch of imagination to accept that interpretation.

The Bible says, "A thousand years is as a day with the Lord, and a day as a thousand years."

No man ever lived one of God's 1,000 year days, not even Methusaleh.

Astrology is the measure of all Biblical time.

The Bible counts a day for a year. The Astrologer counts a day for a year, and nobody else counts time in that way.

The Zodiac is three hundred and sixty degrees and it has been the Astronomer's pendulum for ages past, until quite recently.

Times, time and a half a time is a Scriptural way of counting. Thus a time is 360 years, times 720 years, a half a time 180 years, making 1,260 years for time, times and a half a time, Zodiac years, of 360 days.

The Zodiac is divided into signs, degrees, minutes and seconds.

The Sun passes through the great Zodiac about every 26,000 years, or he is a little over 2,000 years in a sign. Thus we will find the Sun passes through one fire, one water and one earth sign in about 6,000 years, or one of God's weeks of work. Then he finishes or ends his work and rests on the 7th, or the air sign. There are three of the periods to each trip of the Sun.

The air signs are great spiritual signs, and spirits are able to converse with man very clearly, not only to converse with man, but when the Sun passes through Libra actually to walk, talk and cohabit with man.

As we must start somewhere, and as the great circuit of the Sun constitutes one period, we will start after the great judgment about to take place.

Each air sign is 1,000 years millinum or Sunday of rest, and then a period of judgment, therefore the period between the judgment and the next Monday morning is pergatory, or a place of second trial. Those not fit to go to a higher sphere must go to hades, where the worm dieth not.

The Sun entering Capricornus gives 2,000 years, when again a portion of the souls of just men will have a chance to go to a higher sphere, but those who have not learned to overcome and control themselves will have no other opportunity of graduation, until the Sun has passed through Capricornus, Sagittarius and Scorpio and entered the Sunday or air sign Libra Very few are able to graduate except at the 26,000 year periods.

The Earth changes its poles twice during the Sun's great trip, once while the Sun passes through Sagittarius and Scorpio and once while it passes through Gemini and Taurus. This brings the snow and ice of the poles under the direct rays of the Sun and causes tremendous floods. These floods come at the close of the polar change, or as the Sun goes out of Taurus or northern side of the Zodiac, and at the beginning of the change at the southern side of the Zodiac, or as the Sun enters the sign Sagittarius. The floods at the southern side of the Zodiac are evidently much larger than those at the northern side, and it must have been about 20,000 years ago that the continent of Atlantas was lost.

The reader will observe that on a hot summer's day, when a cloud of moisture surrounds the earth, the heat is almost unbearable, and vegetation springs spontaneously from the ground, and worms and insect life thrive and increase rapidly.

In consequence of the intense heat, great growths of vegetable matter and prolific insect life are tho result. The period of the Sun's passage through Sagittarius and Scorpio it was called "Hades or Hell, where the worm dieth not."

Such a place would be a very undesirable place to live. None but those who could not overcome habits, desires and temper would have to go there..

We must now stop to bring up a little proof of this.

In the 49th chapter of Genesis, where Jacob blesses his twelve sons, he is really giving the attributes of the twelve signs of the Zodiac.

I have shown elsewhere that the Bible says the story of Abraham is an allegory, and, notwithstanding we have the Jews with us, it is a question whether there ever was an Abraham or twelve tribes of Israel. Mind, I do not say there was not. But if the story of Abraham was an allegory, the story of Christ would have to be an ellegory, as he was the seed of Abraham.

Jacob in blessing his sons spake of the elder, Reuben, first, and here we have names given and even the names of the mothers, so it would seem rediculous to claim there was no such people.

In giving the attributes of the Zodiac, Jacob assigns his eldest son to Libra, which was formerly the ascending sign of the Zodiac, and then goes back.

ward on through the signs the same as the Sun seems to go annually.

1. Son, Reuben, which means "behold a son." Born of Leah. Assigned to Libra.

2. Son, Simeon, which means "listening.'." Born of Leah. Assigned to Scorpio.

3. Son, Levi, which means crown wreath, or success. Born of Leah. Assigned to Sagittarius.

4. Son, Judah, means praised. Born of Leah. Assigned to Capricornus.

5. Son, Dan, means to judge. Born of Bilhah, Rachel's maid. Assigned to Aquarius.

6. Son, Naphtali, means wrestling. Born of Bilhah, Rachel's maid. Assigned to Pisces.

7. Son, Gad, means a troop or overcomers. Born of Zilpah, Leah's maid. Assigned to Aries.

8. Son, Ashar, means happiness. Born of Zilpah, Leah's maid. Assigned to Taurus.

9. Son, Issachar, means he is hired. Born of Leah and assigned to Gemini.

10. Son, Zebulun, means habitation. Born of Leah. Assigned to Cancer.

11. Son, Joseph, means "He shall add." Born or Rachel. Assigned to Leo.

12. Son, Benoni, means calamity; changed to

Benjamin, meaning son of the right hand, or success. Born of Rachel  Assigned to Virgo.

As we must go the other way around the Zodiac,
we will give the verse and attirbutes of the signs,
including the history of man's religion.

Some might claim that this history of religion
was made to fit into the Zodiac, but this claim
would be very foolish, as the symbols of the Zodiac
are found engraved on the pyramids and oblisks of
Egypt and temples of India, which antedate all other
recorded history, and the Bible is an Astrological
work, without doubt.

Gen., 49th chapter, 5-6 verses, gives attributes to
Simon and Levi, or Scorpio and Sagittarius together,
as one.

5. Simon and Levi are brothers; instruments of
cruelty are in their habitations.

6. Oh, my soul, come not thou into their secret.
Into their assembly, mine honor, be not thou united,
for in their anger they slew a man, and in their self
will they digged down a wall.

7. Cursed be their anger, for it was fierce, and
their wrath for it was cruel. I will divide them in
Jacob and scatter them in Israel.

This is the kind of people who could not graduate
and had to go into hades—i. e., take another term of
school of 26,000 years.

People born of these two signs are the most intensely hot tempered of any of the twelve signs.
While they are admirable people and try hard to
be good citizens, their faults are of that peculiar
order of lack of self control, it requires patience to
overcome.

As the snow and ice gathered at the poles again
and earth began to cool, reptilion life became very
strong and undoubtedly the spirits of men were even

able to take possession of the lower animals, especially as the Sun passed over into the sign Libra.

I have before called attention to the fact that all
is mind and consequently all things must have souls
and spiritual bodies, hence the lower animals are
but little lower than man, and the serpent could
talk.

We judge of man's intelligence by his wants and
his means of supplying his wants. Then who can
draw the line for the immortal soul has the very
wise man got it and the next not or has he got it
and the next not, and so on down the line. Or has
your cannibal got a soul and the domestic animal,
who is a better companion, who wants your society,
rather than his kind, not got a soul? Then the tree
and plant show intelligence and of course they have
souls, and we may go still farther, the atoms seek
each other when combustion takes place, which
shows intelligence there.

The Bible is full of Spiritualism and even John,
4th and 1st verse, says, "Brothers, try the spirits
whether they are of God or not."

Are they not all of God?

Certainly, but some are not fit for associations.
These were the kind Christ is said to have cast out
of the insane man of Gadarenes and others. I have
said, when the Sun is in the air signs, Spiritualism
grows strong. When the Sun entered Libra "the
Sons of God saw that the daughters of men were
fair to look upon and they took them wives." Genesis 6.

Here the Spirits really materialized and cohabited with man.

While the Sun passed through Libra the Earth
was comparatively new, in this renovation, and men
lived to be very old and got very wise.

In man's wisdom he saw the only way out of hades

was through evolution and reincarnation, consequently 16,000 years ago sex worship began.

What other reason could there be for worshiping the sex functions, except the one given above, and this is the oldest religion we have any record of. Let us see what Jacob says of Reuben.

Gen. 49-3. "Reuben, thou art my first born, my might, and the beginning of my strength, the excellency of dignity, and the excellence of power.

Fourth verse. Unstable as water, thou shalt not excel because thou wentest up to thy father's bed, then defilest thou it. He went up to my couch."

Remember, it was these people who cohabited with spirits, defiled the couch of God.

Also remember the sign Libra lost its position as the ascendant. Well, people born in that sign are nearly always of such beauty they well might tempt the Gods; they hold the marriage vows lightly, have frequent spells of melancholy and sadness as if mourning for the lost position on the ascendant. They are very wise people, yet with all of this wisdom they seldom excel in anything. Yet a more trustworthy, noble people is not produced in any of the signs.

As the Sun goes out of a sign the influence of the sign is carried to an extreme. Consequently sex worship ran into lust worship.

As the Sun passed over into Virgo, the extreme of lust worship ran into Virgin worship.

We have now started the Monday morning of another of God's weeks.

Genesis 49-27, Jacob says: "Benjamin shall ravin as a wolf; in the morning he shall devour the prey, and at night he shall divide the spoil."

There is nothing particular in this only the bitterness of fanatical justice and virtue.

# INFLUANCE OF THE 12 SIGNS OF THE ZODIAC

## OR

## ASTROLOGY AND RELIGION

TRUE HISTORY OF ALL RELIGIONS OF THE WORLD, THE STORY
OF THE OLD AND NEW TESTIMENT, THE STORY OF THE SUN GOD,
AND THE STORY OF THE SON OF GOD IN THE GREAT ZODIAC.
THE STORY OF THE CHRISTIAN RELIGION INACTED BY THE SUN
AND STARS EVERY YEAR. IS IT A PROOF OF THE TRUITH OF THE
CHRISTIAN RELIGION? STARTLING! INTRESTING! WONDERFUL!
THE GREAT CROSS ON WHICH THE SUN GOD IS CRUCIFIED.

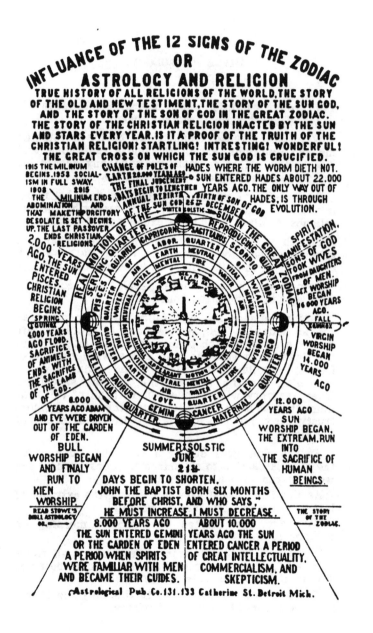

1915 THE MILINUM BEGINS. 1953 SOCIALISM IN FULL SWAY.
1908  2015
THE MILINUM ENDS

CHANGE OF POLES OF EARTH 20.000 YEARS AGO.
THE FINAL JUDGEMENT
DAYS BEGIN TO LENGTHEN
ANNUAL REBIRTH
BIRTH OF SON OF GOD
OF THE SUN GOD 25 of DECEMBER
WINTER SOLSTIC

HADES WHERE THE WORM DIETH NOT.
SUN ENTERED HADES ABOUT 22.000
YEARS AGO. THE ONLY WAY OUT OF
HADES, IS THROUGH EVOLUTION.

THE ABOMINATION AND THAT MAKETH DRGITORY DESOLATE IS SET UP. THE LAST PASSOVER ENDS CHRISTIAN RELIGIONS

2.000 YEARS AGO. THE SUN ENTERED PISCES. CHRISTIAN RELIGION BEGINS.

SPRING EQUINOX 4.000 YEARS AGO FLOOD. SACRIFICE OF ANIMELS ENDS WITH THE SACRIFICE OF THE LAMB OF GOD.

REAL MOTION OF THE SUN IN THE GREAT ZODIAC

SERVING QUARTER  REPRODUCING QUARTER
LABOR QUARTER
EARTH  NEUTRAL
MENTAL  FIRE
VITAL  MENTAL
WEALTH
WISDOM
INTELLECTUAL QUARTER
MATERNAL QUARTER

PISCES  AQUARIUS  CAPRICORN  SAGITTARIUS  SCORPIO
ARIES  LIBRA
TAURUS  VIRGO
GEMINI  CANCER  LEO

SPIRIT MANIFESTATION.
SONS OF GOD
TOOK WIVES FROM DAUGHTERS OF MEN.
SEX WORSHIP BEGAN 16.000 YEARS AGO.

FALL EQUINOX
VIRGIN WORSHIP BEGAN 14.000 YEARS AGO

8.000 YEARS AGO ADAM AND EVE WERE DRIVEN OUT OF THE GARDEN OF EDEN.
BULL WORSHIP BEGAN AND FINALY RUN TO KIEN WORSHIP.

READ STOWE'S BULL ASTROLOGY OL.—

SUMMER SOLSTIC JUNE 21st

DAYS BEGIN TO SHORTEN.
JOHN THE BAPTIST BORN SIX MONTHS BEFORE CHRIST, AND WHO SAYS,"
HE MUST INCREASE, I MUST DECREASE.

8.000 YEARS AGO THE SUN ENTERED GEMINI OR THE GARDEN OF EDEN A PERIOD WHEN SPIRITS WERE FAMILIAR WITH MEN AND BECAME THEIR GUIDES.

12.000 YEARS AGO SUN WORSHIP BEGAN. THE EXTREAM, RUN INTO THE SACRIFICE OF HUMAN BEINGS.

THE STORY OF THE ZODIAC.

ABOUT 10.000 YEARS AGO THE SUN ENTERED CANCER A PERIOD OF GREAT INTELLECTUALITY, COMMERCIALISM, AND SKEPTICISM.

Astrological Pub. Co. 131.133 Catherine St. Detroit Mich.

People born under the strong influence of Virgo are very peculiar, especially about their food, and they are quite old maidish and cannot eat when excited. The ladies generally have large, soulful eyes and look very innocent. It is hard for them to fix their affections and harder to express them, hence there are many old maids among them or they marry late in life.

The extreme of virgin worship ran into sacrificing virgins to the gods, and burning the widows on the funeral pile, of which we still have a relic.

Of course, as the Sun came out of Virgo into Leo, where the Sun was the most powerful, and the sign which astrologers say he rules, and they call the Sun the father, the Moon the mother, so the Son is here born of the Virgin. This by the way of the Sun's passage through the great Zodiac.

With the Sun's passage over into Leo 12,000 years ago Sun worship began, and as I have shown, a sign casts a shadow in the signs of its own domain, and its reflections in its opposite sign, we get an expression of Sun worship in Aries or in Abraham's time. I shall now show the God of Abraham and Jacob was the Sun.

Joseph is assigned to Leo, and Jacob in blessing him says, 49th chapter, verse 22: "Joseph is a fruitful bough, even a fruitful bough by a well, whose branches run over the wall."

The Sun is a fruitful bough. He is the life giver. He rules Leo.

In Joseph's dream his father, mother and eleven brothers bowed down to him. August is the harvest month; the Sun, Moon and eleven signs of the Zodiac all yield their bounties to Leo (Joseph) or August, where the Sun is annually the strongest. This fills the whole bill.

Is. 40-10: "Behold, the Lord will come with a strong hand, and his arm shall rule for him; behold, his reward is with him, and his work before him."

This is the Sun. His reward is with him and his work before him.

In this Joseph becomes the wheat gatherer for Pharoah. Without a stretch of imagination, this fits the place.

Psalms 147-7: "Sing unto the Lord with thanksgiving; sing praises upon the harp unto our God. Who covereth the heavens with clouds, who prepareth rain for the earth, who maketh grass to grow upon the mountains."

This is surely the Sun, "Who sendeth rain on the just and unjust alike."

Amos 9-5: "And the Lord God of Hosts is he that toucheth the land and it shall melt, and all that dwell therein shall mourn: and it shall rise up wholly like a flood, and shall be drowned, as by the flood of Egypt."

This is surely the Sun in the spring of the year that causeth the frozen ground to melt and spring floods to take place.

They speak of the most high God and the Sun is the highest of the solar system, and each sign of the Zodiac is called a house or mansion in the skies, so "In my father's house there are many mansions."

Every sign is a mansion in the skies presided over by a Lord, one of the Sun's satellites, but the Sun is the chief, "The most high God."

The people born in Leo partake of the nature of Joseph or the Sun. They are fruitful; that is, they can adapt themselves to any position in life they chance to get into, and are very mechanical and inventive; can do anything they try to do. Nine times out of ten a lady born in this sign, if she wants man's work done, will not wait for a man to come and do it but will take hold and do it herself.

Webster will tell you that even the days of the week are named after the planets, Sunday after the Sun.

How many people know that we have been observing Sunday as a day of rest and religious worship, because an Astrologer gave it to the world? Here is Constantine's edict:

"Constantine, Emperor Augustus, to Helfidius: On the venerable day of the Sun let the magistrates and people residing in the cities rest and let all workshops be closed. In the country, however, persons engaged in agriculutre may freely and lawfully continue their pursuits; because it often happens that another day is not so suitable for grain sowing or for vine planting, lest by neglecting the proper moment for such operations the bounty of Heaven be lost. Given the 7th day of March, Crispus and Constantine being Consuls each of them for the second time."

March 7th, A. D. 321, Constantine issued this famous edict, which has made Sunday a day of religious service ever since.

The venerable day of the Sun and the expression that the proper moment for vine planting, and so forth, might be lost, is astrological.

The ancients called the Sun and satellites Lords and assigned them to the days of the week and named them as follows:

The Sun, Michael, ruled Sunday.

The Moon, Gabriel, Monday.

Mars, Samuel, Tuesday.

Mercury, Raphael, Wednesday.

Jupiter, Sachiel, Thursday.

Venus, Annel, Friday.

Saturn, Cassiel, Saturday.

Now you have had the Sun born of the virgin, and finally Sun worship with its extreme, the sacrificing of thousands of human beings to the Sun. As the Sun passes out of the sign Leo in Cancer, symbolized by the crab, which crawls backward, the extreme runs to infidelity or disbelief.

The people born in this mental sign are very intellectual, and at that time they became disgusted with the fanatical bloody sacrifice of human beins, so they entered a period going backwards so far as religion was concerned; they telerated no particular form of religion, but were fully as much wrapt up in commercial life as we are now, but fare moro. humain and kindly disposed to one another. Judging by the sign, they could not have expressed tho hypocrisy and selfishness we do in our cycle.

The whole period was a period of rapid advancement of mankind from a worldly standpoint.

Genesis 49-13 says: "Zebulum shall dwell at tho haven of the sea; and he shall be for a haven of ships; and his border shall be unto Zidon."

"Zidon" means fishing.

People born in the sign Cancer are exceptionally bright people, good at business, manufacturing, farming, in fact, in any kind of business, and yet seldom get rich. They believe in giving everybody a chance to make a living, but do not encourage pauperism or begging.

They should never get far away from large bodies of water.

They are more successful in games of chance than people born in other signs, also in fishing, or where there is an element of chance in it.

They are always very skeptical.

We get the best clairvoyants from this sign and the ladies make the best of wives and mothers.

As the Sun passed out of Cancer there was little toleration of any religious belief, so as the Sun

passed into Gemini, another air sign, spirit manifestation became very strong again.

Of course there will always be a relic of a former
civilization remain over after a great change, just
as you still have a relic of sex worship in Mormonism, and there was in this case a relic of very
religious people.

From the fanatical religionist of Leo, clear
through Cancer, remained a large body of people
who willingly put themselves under spiritual guidance and called themselves a chosen people. The
old writers called these Adam and Eve, but forgot
to tell you where the people came from that enabled Cain to go to the land of Nod and take himself a wife. This he did by going back to the people
who were not under spirit guidance.

Going backwards is one of the greatest sins before

God, hence there can be no truth to the idea of
transmigration of souls into the lower animals; but
the tendency is always upward.

Remember, we get nothing of Adam and Eve except as they were being driven out of the Garden
of Eden.

The Sun entered the sign Cancer 10,000 years ago
entered Gemini about 8,000 years ago.

The Bible writers give a brief hint as to former
conditions and leave it to future astrologers to read
between the lines or from astrological truths, as I
am now doing.

While they speak of the spirit controls as God's,
not in the singular God, and they give to them the
attributes of men. These Gods make mistakes, get
very angry, are defeated in their purpose by men;
in fact, they are men, without the body of flesh.

Think of the Great God of the Universe, who
makes nothing in vain, getting angry and slaying
4,000 of his chosen people, and would have slain all

but for one of his poor, weak mortals coaxing him off. See Exodus XXXII.

Of course this is an illustration to show the folly of looking backward, as did the spirits who cohabited with man, when the Sun was in Libra, or as they did when they ate of the forbidden fruit in the Garden of Eden, or Gemini, as expressed in the desires of the children of Israel when they cried to go back to the fleshpots of Egypt. Exodus XVI. Or as did Lot's wife. Everything goes to show the forbidden fruit is a lust for follies, once broken away from by men.

Then again think of the God of the Universe at the prayers of man helping them slay one another, and he was with them and they succeeded in the mountains, but they could not succeed in the valleys because their opponents had chariots of iron.

Judges 1-19: "And the Lord was with Judah, and he drove out the inhabitants of the mountain, but could not drive out the inhabitants of the valley, because they had chariots of iron."

That this applied to the great God of the Universe would be rediculous, but what astrological meaning is attached to it I have not yet solved. The careful reader will find the Bible full of such unreasonable things when taught from the old orthodox standpoint, but which becomes perfectly rational when viewed from the astrological point of view.

As before stated, it is a grand, glorious time to live while the Sun passes through the air signs, therefore this was a period of a Garden of Eden. But the Sun must go out of the sign, yet during the time the Sun was in the sign the people were very obedient to their spirit guides.

Jacob's blessing says, Gen. 49-14: "Issachar is a strong ass, crouching down between two burdens."

Verse 15: "And he saw that rest was good, and the land that it was pleasant; and bowed his shoulder to bear, and became a servant unto tribute."

Gemini is the first of the intellectual quarter, and as soon as the Sun passed out of Gemini, man was left, by the spirits, to his own resources.

I think I hear the reader inquire what about the "forbidden fruit." All right; we find Gemini people as docile as the ass; obedient,. but alive to their interests; willing to work, generally not satisfied with one line of trade, but must carry a burden on both shoulders, as they fill every description Jacob has given.

Forbidden fruit was, this society must not do what the Libra people did, cohabit with the spirits or become licentious or resort to permiscuity among themselves.

They failed to overcome their weaknesses and went back to sex worship, so as the Sun went out of Gemini, 6,000 years ago, it went into the vital earth sign Taurus, symbolized by the bull. They were then told: "Go out now, and replenish the earth."

Had they been able to overcome they could even have overcome death itself, but that was not to be. They had to be cast out as the Sun must go into Taurus. They saw their weakness and clothed themselves against the conditions as best they could. This the old writer called fig leaves.

Taurus is a luxuriant pleasure loving sign.

Jacob's blessing, 49-20, says: "Out of Asher his bread shall be fat, and he shall yield royal dainties."

Taurus people are very sympathetic, kind and sunny tempered, until you try to drive them, and then they are as contrary as a bull.

Peculiarities of people born in this sign are the end of the first finger is generally a quarter of an inch below the nail of the second finger. If this occurs on the hand of people born in other signs, you will find they had Tauris rising, or the Moon,

Mars or several other planets in Taurus. · This in-
variably denotes a person easily persuaded.

As Gemini is the shadow of Libra, so is Taurus
the shadow of Virgo, sex worship was here shadowed
by the worship of the bull, which was a companion
and aid to man in "earning his bread by the sweat
of his brow."

Egypt worshiped the white bull Apies. China,
Japan, Scandinavia, all worshiped the bull.

Finally the Sun drew near to Aries, bull worship
run into cow worship, and finally to the heifer, or
virgin cow, in shadow of the Virgo influence, which
is also an earth sign.

While the people of Taurus are the most sunny
tempered people, they are also the most stubborn
people when they take a thing into their head, so
just as the bull must be made a stag before he
becomes manageable, the spirit of the people had to
be broken by a flood caused by the change of the
earth's poles, though this change is not so fierce as
that on the other side of the Zodiac.

Thubin as pole star gives way easier than Polarius.

It is a mistake to suppose the whole earth was
drowned; but the story of the ark landing on Mount
Arrat is but an allegory of the comparatively few
who found shelter on mountain tops.

Two days of God's third week have gone when the
Sun enters Aries about 4,000 years ago. Bull worship held over and, as I stated, run into cow and
then the virgin cow or heifer worship. Adrian built
the temple of Venus on Mount Calvary, which was
named in honor of Calva, the Kine name of Venus.
Juno, Venus and Isces were symbols of their Kine
Gods.

Let us remember virgin worship run into terrible
sacrifices of virgins to the Gods, which was carried
on in Leo to terrific slaughter of human beings to

the Sun God. As the Sun passed over into Aries, which, like Leo, is a fire sign, and the shadow of Leo, heifer worship had run into sacrificing cow virgins, and Josephus in telling of the wonders of that time said, a heifer when being led to the sac- rifice gave birth to a lamb. The Sun had entered the sign of the lamb, so now you get the sacrificing of lambs to the Gods.

Remember, Abraham was about to slay his own son when the angel showed him a ram with his horns entangled in the brush. This lamb sacrificing went on until the sacrificing of the lamb of God we have heard so much about.

While there is strong evidence to show the story of Abraham and the twelve tribes of Israel, including the story of Christ, are mythical, that no such char- acters existed, there is positive evidence to show that the peculiarities of the various forms of wor- ship were induced by the Sun's passage through the different signs of the Zodiac. In that case, why should there not have been a real individual Christ, a personal being?

Everything points to a great intelligent power ruling through evolution and reincarnation, and if there is such it is but natural that there was a per son called the Son of God. At least, there is no harm in believing it, and the grand ideal character must be a help to man to overcome.

Jacob in blessing his seventh son says, Genesis 49-19: "Gad, a troop shall overcome him, but he shall overcome at the last."

Aries people are natural overcomers; they are a terror to their enemies. The tribe of Gad were said to be great warriors.

Christ represented óne who had overcome him- self.

"He that overcomes his spirit is greater than he that takes a city, greater than the mighty."

I do not care what others say. I prefer to believe there was an individual Christ, but I also believe Astrology is the true basis of all religion.

When writing of this and thinking of this grand character I can hardly keep from shouting Hallelujah with my old brother Methodists, with whom I once trained, until I outgrew their forms and beliefs as they outgrew Catholocy or other forms of religion.

Christ died as the Sun passed over from the sign of the lamb into the sign of the fishes.

Christ spoke of the fearful times that were to come in regard to hypocrisy in religious beliefs.

The sign Pisces is ruled over by Jupiter, the God of wealth, and for the past 2,000 astrological years we have had the worship of the almighty dollar a truly commercial period. Christ sent the fishermen to catch a fish which had money in its mouth, in type of this sign of the fishes. He also selected his disciples from among the fishermen. The Sun rules Sunday and annually passes (in appearance) through the sign of the fishes, in token of which we celebrate Lent and eat fish one day of the week in honor to the Sun and the sign of the fishes.

Jupiter, the God of wealth, rules this sign, and the typical Church of Christendom was built in honor of Jupiter. This is St. Peter's Church at Rome. St. Peter himself was the chief of the fishermen.

We shall find every type fulfilled here.

For the past 2,000 years we have had the commercialism of the shadow of the water sign, Cancer, without the virtues that great mental sign gave, but with all of the propensities for fishing for money.

Christ said: "It is easier for the camel to go through the eye of a needle than for a rich man to enter into the Kingdom of Heaven."

Ezekiel XXII, God says to the Jews: "Thou hast taken usury and increase and thou hast greedily gained of thy neighbors, and I have smitten my hand against you, and ye shall be scattered among the heathen and among the countries until thy filthy. ness is consumed out of thee."

They stand scattered today as an evidence of it.

The only time that Christ ever used force or sanc tioned the use of force was when he scourged the money changers from the temple. But what have we had for the past 2,000 years but the money gathering shadow of Cancer and the reflection in hypocrisy from Virgo.

Let us not forget Aries gave us the shadow of Leo, but instead of sacrificing human beings to the Sun, they sacrificed lambs and finally the lamb of God.

Aries gave us the reflection of Libra, but instead of sex worship we found a plurality of wives and concubines as represented by King Solomon and King David. But what do you get from Virgo to the cold water sign Pisces? You get pretentions and hypocrisy, a pretention to abhor more than one wife, and then having a half dozen women on the side, or else debauching some other man's wife. The ministers assail Mormonism and then, accord- ing to the book entitled "CRIMES OF PREACH- ERS," 26 per cent of them are criminals and most of their crimes are against the opposite sex. Yet we cannot blame the church for this, and we should pity rather than blame good men for falling where temptations are naturally with the flesh all of the time.

In parallel to the above let us look at our false money gathering system. "Take thou no usury or increase," says the Scriptures. Yet every effort of man is for great gains, to become immensely rich. No matter what suffering it entails, no matter how many prisons and poorhouses are filled, no matter how many murders are committed to keep in the swim, no matter how many little children are dwarfed in mind and body by being dragged to the workshop, instead of found in the nursery or school-room, no matter how many hearts are wrung, we must get rich quick.

No man could earn half a million dollars in a life-time, yet through our robbery system we have men worth hundreds of millions of dollars, and the church supports the system and opposes socialism or gov-ernment and municipal ownership.

Stop and think; money and property never cre-ated anything. It has no feeling. It does not wear clothes, or have to eat to live. It has not even an alementary canal or an organ to experience pain. Yet all of your laws are created to defend property, an inanimate thing, and none in defense of man, who must create all wealth.

A man may leave his jackass a million dollars, in trust, and in the name of the jackass fund that million dollars will go on beating down wages and robbing labor.

Your laws are made in the interest of trusts and corporations, and manipulated for those who have the most money, until your courts are a farce and your laws a menace to the rights and interests of the people. It has become a byword, "There is no justice in law."

The man who wins a law suit, unless the sum is very large, will lose more than the amount involved.

I, myself, was held up and robbed of $500 by a so-called court of equity. (God save the mark.)

This was money I needed in my old age, but what did they care for that?. Though aged and feeble, I am compelled to set much of the type in this book, and I am not a practical printer.

That the reader may know the decision was not a criminal matter, I will state it was an insurance

matter, and the supreme court reversed the decis
ion in another identical case of the same lot. But
I did not have money to carry my case higher, and
the court that robbed me did not make restitution,
which an honorable citizen who saw his error would
have done. There is much more that would make
the matter look blacker did space allow of explanation.

I was even deceived by my own lawyer, and this
is not the only time I have been wronged by the system that should have protected me.

I do not like to write so bitterly, as I know some
of these men are gentlemen in everything else; but
they cannot be honorable in a system so bad that
one of the fathers of his country, Thomas Jefferson,
said, "The seeds of national dissolution will be
found in our judiciary system." When, never getting anything but wrong from a system I fought
to uphold, how can I have any more respect for it
than I would for a band of pirates?

Lawyers wer created to evade law, not to enforce
it, and I do not believe it possible to find an honest
lawyer in his practice.

All history shows the profession one of disrepute.
Back in the seventeenth century, in England, the
lawyers became so numerous they became a pest,
on purpose causing disputes, to make business for
themselves, and it became necessary to suppress
them and limit their number. Quoted from John
Evlin's diary.

Today the whole world is in the hands of lawyers.
You cannot elect a judge except he be a lawyer.
The most of your legislators are lawyers. The people seem crazy to honor lawyers. This should not
be. It is said a lawyer cannot be an honest man.

I once attended a meeting of the wise men of the
world and a president of a law college was introduced to address the assembly, when an old gentle-

man arose and asked the privilege of a question.

Said he: · "We are called the wise men of the world, and we believe it is impossible for a lawyer to be an honest man. I would like the opinion of the president of a law college. Do you think it is possible for a lawyer to be an honest man?"

The speaker hesitated a moment and then scratched his head, and drawled out in a humorous strain: "Y-e-s, i-f h-e d-o-e-s n-o-t p-r-a-c-t-i-c-e l-a-w."

Peter the Great was once in London, England, and on visiting the courts he asked his escort, "Who are all these men in gowns and wigs?" The answer was "Lawyers."

"Well, well," said Peter, "I have but three lawyers in the whole of Russia, and I shall behead two of them as soon as I reach home."

It was a lawyer that tempted Christ.

Luke X-25: "And behold, a certain lawyer stood up and tempted him, saying, Master, what shall I do to inherit eternal life?"

Verse 26: "He said unto him, What is written in the law? How readest thou it?"

Verse 27: "And he answering said, Thou shalt love the Lord thy God with all thy heart, and with all thy soul, and with all thy strength, and with all thy mind, and thy neighbor as thyself."

Who thinks of his neighbor, where his own pocket is concerned, except to fill that pocket at his neighbor's expense?

XI-46: "And he said, Woe unto you also, ye lawyers! for ye lade men with burdens grievous to be borne, and ye yourselves touch not the burdens with one of your fingers."

This is a judge-cursed land. We have over 60,000 judges from justice courts to supreme bench, all receiving from $1,500 to $10,500 per year. This is many times more than they could earn at anything

else, or they would not take such risks and rottenness in politics to get the office.

Ask any man on the street if there is any law for
a poor man and he will laughingly say, "Yes, lots of
law, but no justice."

So your courts have become a farce, a byword,
and there is no justice for a man without money,
and the State cannot convict a scoundrel with
money; or if it did, he would have a soft place for
a few weeks and then be pardoned.

The public will soon look upon the captain of
industry, whose success has been established on ·a
foundation of child labor, as a goal.

Upon the members of corporations and trusts as
pirates.

Upon bankers, judges and lawyers as confidence
operators.

The public should establish a system of settling
disputes by a board of arbitration chosen by both
sides and a third selection by the arbitrators. Such
settlement should be made legal. If this were done
we would not have expensive courts and legal professional thieves, with cases dragging for months,
and sometimes years, at an outrageous expense to
the people.

Then burn the law books, most of which have been
created by bribery in the interest of unprincipled
wealth gatherers.

All of this is due to our false and terrible cut-throat
competitive system.

Take the meanest banker that ever bribed a con-
gressman or foreclosed a mortgage. The vilest judge
that ever yielded a case to influence, the meanest
lawyer that ever sold out a client, or the worst saloon
keeper that ever wrung the last dime from a custo-
mer whose starving children cried for bread, or the
burglars that cracked a safe, and with the ex-

ceptional degenerate these men at times are kindhearted gentlemen. It is the false systems and th'e
honor extended to wealth and to professions which
are a crime before God, which are to blame for our
troubles.

It is a crime to uphold this false system in the face
of suffering humanity.

All of our customs, as well as our laws, are in the
interest of wealth and the successful.

If we see a team with a large horse and a small
one, we will raise a row mighty quick, if the small
horse has not been given the long end of the evener.
But it is not so with human beings. We give all of
the advantage to the fortunate man, and throw
every obstacle in the way of the poor and unfor-
unate.

Moneyed men declare a socialistic system would
stop all progress, talent and ambition. But how is it
today? The man with small capital stands no chance
in the race with he of a large capital, who is able to
buy privileges the poor man can never get; natural
talent stands no show with money. It is a rare instance
where genius does arise, but when it does, in spite of
all obstacles, a great adieu is made about it, as if the
system had helped instead of hindered him.

It is not considered good taste to speak of one's
own affairs, in a book like this, but when referring
to conditions it is better to give experience than
hearsay.

Let us see whether genius or merit stands a show
with the moneyed classes, under this competitive
system. I will first cite my own experience. I am a
descendant of John Stow, the Antiquarian, whose
works today are considered almost indispensible to
any moderately furnished English library.

(The name was originally spelled Stow, my own
father spelled his name that way; younger generations have added the final "e.")

The Stows, the Beachers and the Lymans were three families who married and intermarried until nearly every family of Stowes will contain a Lyman or a Beecher, and every family of Beechers will contain a Stow or a Lyman, and in every family of Lymans will be found a Stow and a Beecher.

All of the families possess one or more literary geniuses.

Though handicapped by the lack of an early education, I naturally took to literary work, but could never get a publisher to publish my productions except where they did not net me a cent.

I finally took to publishing my work myself, but it is one thing to write and publish and another thing to get the work on the market. I have found that if I can only get a reader for one of my books, that reader will soon be applying for other of my books until he has read them all, and I have been called on for twenty copies of the same book by the same reader, at different times, because he was so pleased and so anxious to have others read the work he would give his copy away and send for another. I have many letters of thanks and congratulations, with such words of commendation as "I consider you one of the deepest thinkers and ablest writers of our times, and no flattery intended." And yet I cannot get publishers to take up my work, and why?

I know other authors who have the same difficulty. Dr. Kleindienst, an old gentleman of Detroit, has several books in manuscript that I know to be worth a thousand times more than the majority of the trash published, in fact they fairly bristle with quaint humor, which could not help but please the reader, yet he suffers in want, and he cannot get a publisher to touch his work, while the most of the stories published, long or short, are seemingly a lot of words, without plot, head or tail, stuff torn from the middle of a story and pressed upon a public who does not half like it, but buy a barrel of trash to get a page of

value, because publishers pretend there is a demand
for such stuff.  The only merit in the stuff is it bears
the stamp of a brain stuffed with correct grammar
and spelling, often at the expense of deeper thought.

Why is this so?

There are several reasons:

1st.  Publishers seek to catch the public eye rather
than the public brain, and they neither lead or follow
public taste, they rather ape one another, or seek to
make money by publishing trash, so we get one valuable book to a hundred worthless ones.  Excepting in
the way of mechanical art, our newspapers and magazines are retrograding.

2nd.  Publishers run along the lines of least resist-
ance, so rather publish the work of a brain-stuffed
college graduate, who has no room for thought, or
the product of the son or daughter of money-bags, or
a persn who has gained notoriety, no matter how,
rather than the work of labored thought, because they
think it will sell quicker, or because it costs them
little or nothing.

3rd.  It is often the case the mony-bag will pay a
big price to have his product plcaed before the public,
so publishers can get about all of that class of trash
they want for nothing, or even get paid to take it,
while the work of genius goes begging or never sees
the light of day.

Then you have your great commercial kings who
have built  mighty fortunes on the ruins of plun-
dered labor.  These men seek fame by building mon-
uments for themselves, and so they found libraries
and stock them, with decaying thought thus retard-
ing human progress, discouraging the modern author and starving genius.

In this way your free-for-all system is about as
encuoraging to talent and genius as the sight of
the blak flag of a pirate would be to the captain,
crew and passengers of a crippled merchant ship.

Look at the hardships of genius.

This same ancestor of mine, whose works are now so much in demand. In his day, in 1561, says Potter's Biblical Encyclopedia: "One of the most noteworthy incidents in the history of men of learning, and one that is truly surprising, is the fact that a man like Stow, whose name now stands in the front rank of antiquaries, should have been permitted to pass his declining years in abject poverty. Still more wonderful is the fact that when nearly 80 years of age he was constituted by royal letters patent a public beggar, and he was commended to charity on the ground of his having 'compiled and published divers necessary books and chronicles.'"

Here are a few of the ghosts of wronged and murdered genius, whose decaying bones your Ca - ־ɔ×ɔ6 would give the public to pick, that he may help to strangle or starve modern genius.

## HARDSHIPS OF GENIUS.

"Camoens, the celebrated writer of the "Lusiad," the great Portuguese epic, ended his life, it is said, in an almshouse, and, at any rate, was supported by a faithful black servant, who begged in the streets of London for him.

Milton sold his copyright of "Paradise Lost" for seventy-two dollars, at three payments, and finished his life in obscurity.

Fielding lies in the burying grounds of the English factory at Lisbon, without a stone to mark the spot.

Goldsmith's "Vicar of Wakefield" was sold for a trifle to save him from the grip of the law.

Savage died in a prison at Bristol, where he was confined for a debt of forty dollars.

Chatterton, the child of genius and misfortune, destroyed himself at the age of eighteen, because there were no hopes before him.

The death of Collins was through neglect, first causing mental derangement.

Bentivoglio was refused admittance into a hospital he had erected himself.

Otway, the English dramatist, died prematurely, and through hunger.

Steele, the humorist, lived a life of perfect warfare with the bailiffs.

Tasso, the Italian poet, was often distressed for five shilling.

Paul Borghese had fourteen trades, yet starved to death withal.

Butler lived a life of penury, and died poor.

Plautus, the Roman comic poet, turned a mill.

Bacon lived a life of meanness and distress.

Sir Walter Raleigh died on the scaffold.

Terrance, the dramatist, was a slave.

Dryden lived in poverty and distress.

Cervantes died of hunger.

Spenser died in want."

Homer was a beggar, and Christ, who had no place to lay his head, was crucified.

Such is the reward and help extended to genius, under this false system.

Labor unions have been formed by union of capital, and they force the man of genius and the man of experience down to a level with the clod, so between the upper and neither    millstones, talent, genius and experience is being crushed to earth, so a government ownership of everything could be no worse than the present condition.

Poverty never did much for itself; we must depend upon the honorable rich to help reforms out, and there is enough wise, honorable men among them, but they need teaching as well as the poor.

Could all of the hardened privileged class see the handwriting on the wall, they would hasten to get under cover and not atempt to "SET UP THE ABOMINATION THAT MAKETH DESOLATE." For which they and their posterity will not only lose their property, but their lives, under the rolling wave of human wrath and human progress about to break.

THIS IS NOT GUESS WORK. THIS IS INSPIRATION!

You should read THE GREAT PROPHESY, which is an Astrological interpretation of the books of Daniel and Revelations. Mailed for 25c.

It is true—as much independence and personal liberty as possible should be maintained, for all men are not constituted alike, and the wants of one man supplied might make him happy, and the same amount would mean extreme poverty to another, for it is true that a railroad cannot be built without an engineer and a donkey, yet no sane person would deny the engineer his superior desires and necessities to a donkey. No person would want to lower the standard of the engineer to the donkey or put him in a stall that would be a luxury to the donkey, nor expect him to lower his family to the level of the donkey by bringing the donkey into the house with him. Neither would you expect him to steal the oats from the donkey. It would be the same with any man on a stage between the donkey and engineer.

The present massing of wealth by wealth, or making money breed money will soon destroy our civilization. It is all wrong.

Why was it tha for 1500 years after Christ no person dare openly advocate the taking of interest on money? I answer it was because of the selfishness of the successful few through making money breed money, a few soon owned all of the wealth, and the masses became desperate and refused to defend the cities where they had no interests and the fall of Sodom and Gomorra, of Thebes, of Ninevah, of Sidon and Tyra, of Troy, of Babylon, of Jerusalem and of Rome, awakened such hatred to the System, it was abhorred.

History is repeating itself. Through interest on money, the few are grasping the world and setting the example of trust and greed until the trust has invaded every branch of trade and the price of living is beyond reason. It is not because of the lack of enough, but it is because of the demand of great profits to pay interest and rent, on the one hand and the desire for excessive profits to get rich quick, by hoarding and cold storage, which is robbing the producer and consumer on the other hand.

What is the greatest crime spoken of in the Bible? "The love of money is the root of all evil."

The prophet Nehemiah saw the great evil coming and cried out to his people: "I pray you let us leave off this usury." Neh. v: 10.

"Thou shalt not give him thy money upon usury, nor lend him thy victuals for increase." Leviticus xxv: 37.

"I rebuked the nobles, and the rulers, and said unto them, 'Ye exact usury, every one of his brother.' And I set a great assembly against them." Nehemiah v: 7.

I wonder if our preachers ever rebuke the nobles and the rulers. The Bible tells us how the old prophets rebuked Saul, David, Solomon and others, but do the clergy rebuke the nobles and the politicians of today?

The 22nd chapter of Ezekiel tells you that for taking usury and greedily gaining one of another God drove the Israelites out of the land he had given their fathers for an everlasting inheritance, and they stand scattered today as an evidence of it.

The only time Christ ever used force, or sanctioned the use of force was when with the scourge he drove the money changers from the temple.

After all it is not to individuals that any war sholud be waged, but it is to false systems.

There are only two sources from which real wealth can be produced. The one from natural resources, which gives no man a monopoly, the other is through cultivation of natural resources, which must be through labor.

Wherever wealth is increased through increased demand because of increase of population or other unlooked for causes, should by taxation or other means revert back to the whole people or it partakes of the nature of a privilege, that any free people should oppose.

That one man can produce a great deal more than another is manifest in two ways, one by superiority of physical strength, and the other by superior brain power, he makes his feeble efforts of greater value. But, neither of these powers could alone achieve any great advantage over another, therefore legal privileges are resorted to, but these are so covered by bad loans and worse customs that the masses are deceived by the false system and legal theft is often covered by the term salary, or legal income, whereas it is only a species of class privileges, and the denial that it is class privilege made under the false hope held out that everybody is offered a fair opportunity under this system, where the fact is the genius whose time is given to perfect his knowledge or to make two blades of grass grow where one grew before has no time to perfect himself in the art of gathering wealth, hence the false system of money gathering is corrpting every branch of industry and stage of society until the churches themselves are mere auxiliaries or assistants to deceive the people and make them an easier prey to the succssful "Prdatory rich," as President Roosevelt styled them. This is what is meant in Ephesians vi: 12, "For we wrestle not against flesh and blood, but against principalities, against powers, against the rulers of darkness OF THIS WORLD, against spiritual wickedness in high places."

If the people are determined they will not see this,

and correct the evil, it will correct itself in a manner thousands of times more terrific than the great French Revolution of 1798.

Such a thing is not to be hoped for, not to be desired, but must we be silenced that it may not be averted or may not be modified to some extent at least?

Many would ask, "But, how will you avert it?"

Says Blackstone, the great English law-giver:

"Money is a creation of law, it is a measure of value, by comparison, whereby we ascertain the comparative values of all commodities."

Government alone reserves the right to create all standards of measurement, and as this tool of measurement must be parted with before it can be of service, there is always a great demand for it, and it is made a legal tender to prevent bickering and strife.

In consequence of the demand people are willing to pay a large usage or percent of profit for the usage of money. This formerly was called usury, regardless of the rate paid, but when usury became unpopular the term was changed to interest, and the people deceived.

As money is a creation of law, and law is a creation of the whole people, nobody but a government sholud be permitted to lend money on interest. As money, in the hands of an individual, belongs to him by sole right, he can do with it what he pleases, and to prevent him from so doing would be depriving him of his liberties as well as depriving the man of his liberties who wishes to borrow, but there is a better way out.

The government alone reserves the right to make money and it should make and pay out money for public works until there is not necessarily an idle man in the land, and it should loan money to the people who can give security, and when a properly appointed commission have ascertained there is not a necessary idle man in the land, the average price of 1,000 commodities should be taken and the stoppage of the issuing of money until the average price

of that 1,000 commodities began to fall below that
fixed esa level, when it would be known money is
growing scarce and sacrifice of commodities are being made when the issue should be resumed until the
average prices of that 1,000 commodities arose to
that fixed sea level. If the prices ever rise above
that level of course the volume of money would be
known to increase or demand fall, which is the same
thing, then it should be decreased through reducing
the volume of taxation.

That a thing of such a· well known and gigantic
oppression and wrong as interest on money, and so
positive and far-reaching in its effects, and so forcefully prohibited by Divine law should receive the
sanction of honest men, and  especially  of  the
churches and clergy, is a phenomena of itself, and
shows clearly that some great social upheaval is
imminent.

It is true, gain, strife and war seems the natural
occupation of man, and we all love it and should be
careful how we condemn others for what we ourselves can hardly resist, yet as teachers of men to
neglect our duty is a crime against God, and interest on money is condemned above all other crimes,
yet I think the hording of necessaries of life and
holding them in cold storage until spoiled for greater
profit is a still greater crime.

Since the above was written there seems to be so
strong a tendency to correct existing social and commercial evils, that if continued I shall be more than
pleased to substitute better matter to take the place
of these pessimistic complaints.  But these reforms
did not originate with the church people or with the
wealthy optimistic class, but with the .pessimistic
kickers against existing evils.  Therefore, we must
uphold, against all encroachments, the constitution
of the United States, which says, "The right to free
speech and a free press shall not be abridged."

## PARDON THE ABOVE DIGRESSION.

You ministers of the gospel, you are fighting an imaginary devil, when the real devil is before your eyes and ye heed him not.

You fight against alcoholic drinks as a temptation, when ye know God put a temptation and a tempter in the Garden of Eden that man might develop a character, and ye howl for prohibition when ye know wine will b⁻ drank in heaven.

Mark XIV-25: "Verily I say unto you, I will drink no more of the fruit of the vine, until that day that I drink it new in the kingdom of God."

It is well to teach men to overcome temptations of the flesh, but nine-tenths of the saloonkeepers follow the business because it is the only door open to them, for successful business, and it is far more honorable than the business of the banker, who openly defies the laws of God, who says, "Take thou no usury or increase."

Now let us look at Jacob's blessing of Naphtali, Genesis 49-21:

"Naphtali is a hind let loose; he giveth goodly words." A hind is a deer; let loose he devours all before him, and that is what this age of wealth gatherers are doing.

"He giveth goodly words," and that is what is being done through deception and confidence operating.

The Pisces people are a good and wise people, but given to much sadness, as if they deplored the terrible state of things, and they are great reformers. But the system of goodly words is characteristic of our hypocritical times. The world is run by deception and fraud, until the old showman says, "The people love to be humbugged."

There is little more chance for a business man to be honest than there is for a lawyer to be honest.

In every line of trade we find all kinds of tricks
of trade are resorted to, from the minister's howl
against an imaginary devil or the demon rum, which
is to attract the attention of the people to show
he is doing something, while he leaves the great
criminals and false systems alone, down or up
through every phase of your false competitive system. The spirit of the trust is everywhere; it is
with your corner grocer as well as with your oil or
railroad trust. The corner grocer will howl against
the trust, and then go on the market and rail at the
farmer if he retails to the consumer.

## WHY THE CHURCH FAVORS THE KING AND THE MILLIONAIRE INSTEAD OF THE PEOPLE.

Perhaps it would not be hard to find that the reason
why the Pope, our American Bishop Ireland, and the
churches in general are so opposed to government,
or municipal ownership, or in other words Socialism,
is because of their great individual wealth and the
vast amount of church property untaxed. Why
should those opposed to churches be forced to pay
taxes for those who do believe in them? This is not
the religious rights our Constitution grants us.

Some will say the church should not pay taxes because the church benefits all. This, however, is disputed by the opposers of the church, who claim that
the bigotry of the church retards human progress;
and we know the religious wars of the past have
caused more bloodshed and misery than all other
wars, pestilence and famine put together. Even
under the two great queens the sorrows and misery
cannot be estimated. Bloody Mary caused the death
or loss of 60,000 souls, and Bloody Elizabeth in re-
taliation caused 60,000 more to lose their lives.

These deaths were not merely the sudden deaths
like those slain in modern battle, but many of them

suffered all of the tortures that the ingenuity of man
could inflict—starvation, the rack, the faggot, even
the eyes burned out with red-hot irons.

The soul revolts against dwelling further upon
the curse brought on mankind through differing in
religious belief.

Now, you poor, benighted souls, who are called
upon to add to the wealth of untaxed church property and to add to the wealth of Pope, bishops,
preachers, and over-paid kings and politicians, to say
nothing of being robbed by corporation, trust and
a usurious bonded system, while you are asked to
live on a pittance and promised mansions in heaven
which they have no means of knowing any more
about than you do, look at the following quotation
taken from the "religious" columns of the Detroit
News-Tribune of the date of November 18, 1906:

"A correspondent asks: 'Is it true that the Pope
is immensely wealthy? Is it not rather true that
since losing his temporal power the Papacy is comparatively poor, having to depend on "Peter's pence"
for its support?'

"In answering this question I am dependent on A.
Le Lievre, an English authority in such matters, who
says:

"'In 1901 the Duke of Norfolk offered the Pope—
who did not refuse to accept the money—£12,000 as
Peter's pence.

"'In 1902 Count Adami made a gift to Leo XIII.
of his villa near Chieti; it contained 600 works of
art. The money value of the present was estimated
at £200,000.

"'In 1903 the Irish Catholic gave its readers some
idea of the value of the pontificate as a commercial
asset. When Leo XIII. celebrated the diamond jubi-
lee of his entrance into the priesthood, the gifts
were estimated to be worth more than $25,000,000.
The late Queen Victoria's present consisted of a dia-

mond ring worth $100,000; the German Emperor offered a ruby ring, valued at $750,000; the Czar of Russia gave a golden crozier, worth $250,000; the Emperor of Austria, a golden casket filled with gold ($100,000); and the contributions in gold coin were ·worth $4,000,000.

" 'In 1904 £60,000 went from America to Pius X. Cardinal Satolli, the bearer of the gift, receiving a fee of $10,000 for officiating at a wedding in New York.

" 'The Roman Catholic Bishop Mehler. of Ratisbon, has lately published a book on "Peter's pence." The Pope's income from this source is now about $1,600,000. In the days of fervent faith it averaged 12,000,000 lire. (An Italian lira equals 19½ cents, United States currency.) The expenses of the Vatican palace are as follows: For the pontiff's private use, 500,000 lire; for the cardinals, 700,000 lire; for poor bishops, 460,000 lire; for the perfects of the apostolic palaces, 1,800,000 lire; for the office of secretary of state, 1,000,000 lire; salaries of officials, 1,500,000 lire; for schools and papal charities, $1,200,-000 lire. Total, 7,160,000 lire per annum.' "

How did the kings and wealth gatherers get this wealth, with which to make those great presents? Did not labor have to produce it all? Why should labor, who does not believe in supporting churches, pay the taxes to support untaxed church property, or sleek, well-fed kings, priests and politicians, who can afford to give such magnificent presents, while the real producer of wealth gets a bare but poor subsistence? These wealthy Popes, bishops, preachers, and church supporters are united to prevent the equality that government ownership or Socialism will bring.

If you are pleased to continue to pay for the support of such institutions, while you take yours in promises of mansions in that heaven so beautiful— that heaven which they deny the existence of, by their expressed anxiety to remain here—you have the right, but you have not the right to cause others to suffer it.

Not one of these preachers are willing to swap the certainty of a luxurious life here for that promised heaven, while untold thousands from the ranks of labor and business, through. despondency are driven to suicide.

If you are satisfied with this, go on giving your money to uphold these sacred confidence operators, who oppose Socialism, who care not what your religion is, but who are working for the emancipation of wage slavery, as we a short time since worked for the emancipation of chattel slavery. But do not complain if you are called on to live in squalor and want while they live in ease and luxury on what you earn.

Do they even follow the Master they pretend to adore? No, they do not.

"Go sell what thou hast and give to the poor and then follow Me."

Fancy the Pope, a bishop, or a wealthy churchman selling what he has and giving to the poor.

"Verily, it is easier for the camel to pass the needle's eye than for a rich man to enter the Kingdom of Heaven."

They preach this, but do not follow it, showing they do not believe what they preach.

Take away the genteel life and fat living and see how many will work for nothing in their Master's vineyard.

Young man, government ownership or radical Socialism does not seek to interfere with your religion, unless your religion, through false teaching, so far blunts or destroys your morals as to cause you to support a system that creates millionaires and paupers, or robs the many for the benefit of the few, even to the extent of robbing yourself and family to support an untaxed system whose teachers do not follow what they preach.

Socialism asks you to stop and think, and reason. Have all the religion you like and any kind you like, and above all guard your morals—yes, guard them so close as to refuse to rob yourself, your family, or your brother producers; and point the finger of scorn at that man or that institution that pretends to follow a Master who had no grand church, no place to lay His head, while they roll in ill-begotten wealth and build such elegant untaxed churches that if you go there in patches and rags and without a contribution you will get such a cold shoulder you will soon be glad to turn away. Indeed, they are against government ownership and Socialism. They do not want equality of man. If you had rather be a hog among kings than to see justice and equality of rights of man, go on supporting such institutions and opposing government ownership, on more radical terms than the postoffice, the army and navy and other similar benefits of the general government or municipal ownership. They will gladly trick you with fool talk about political trickery and ignore the rottenness of the politics of the day.

This robbery system is growing worse and worse. There can be only one way out of it, and that is through government, and municipal ownership, in its extreme called Socialism, but in its true religious sense it is to "Love your neighbor as yourself." Yet the church does not take it up, and the Catholic church, from its Vatican, is openly fighting against it.

### HOW WILL IT END?

Remember Christ sent his two fishermen to the man bearing a pitcher of water to tell him the last passover would be celebrated in his house. Well, from the sign of the two fishes the Sun has passed over into Aquarius, the water-bearer.

You will notice Aquarius the water barer is the man baring the pitcher of water spoken of and the sign Pisces or sign of the fishes the fisherman.

For ages the Jews have been celebrating what they supposed was the passover of the Red Sea by the children of Israel, while the Christian church have been celebrating a custom they know not what, while the real passover is the Sun passing over from one sing to another.

This last passover must end our present system, and a better understanding of the true religion will take its place.

In the Millennium Christ is to reign a thousand years, with his Father.

Now look at the colored chart and study it closely. The sign Leo, where Sun worship took place, is right opposite to Aquarius, who receives its reflection.

The planet Uranus, the son of the Sun God, the only one of the Sun's satellites which revolves on its axis in such a peculiar manner, is really the only begotten son of the Sun. He is the Lord of Aquarius, but for ages and ages, like the Son of Man, had no place to lay his head—that is, no house was given him, like the rest of the planets.

Of Neptune we know but little, but there is no doubt he is the "Ancient of days," spoken of.

The planet Saturn was given rule over Aquarius and Capricornus. But he is to be bound for a thousand years.

Saturn is called, by Astrologers, "THE GREAT EVIL." In the Chaldeaic he was called Shetan; in Greek, Tetan, or power; in Babylonia Hebrew Saten. In the modern language our Christian friends call him Satan, and they pretend to fight a spiritual devil and let the devil of selfishness, lust and false systems, go by.

Before we settle down to the millennium, and good will to man, the workshop Christ represented as a carpenter, a builder, must be cleansed, just as you cleanse a carpenter shop Saturday night to have it ready for Monday morning.

Daniel, the prophet and astrologer, said in the last days we shall have such troublous times as was never before known. Great wars are to take place.

Revelations says blood shall flow to the horse bridles.

Does this mean blood shall flow four feet deep? Certainly not. I have been engaged in many very large battles, and I never saw but little patches of blood here and there. Then what is meant?

The constellation Pegacious extends far up into the sign Aquarius, and these wars will last until the Sun reaches the horse neck. Mind you, this does not read horse's neck, but horse neck.

What are these wars to be about?

"The stars shall fall to the earth, like a tree casting its untimely fruit, shaken by a mighty wind."

Does this mean the stars of the heavens, so far distant it has taken 3,000,000 years for their light to reach us? Certainly not; but, as it says, kings, princes and money lords. It is they who will fall, just as they are falling in Russia today.

Every mountain and every island shall be moved out of its course. This is governments.

What, have we not the best government on the face of the earth?

Yes, certainly we have, and the most beautiful flag, and we will defend it with our lives; but we will defend it from evils within, and there can be no greater evil than that system that robs the masses, that which dwarfs the child's mind and body to satisfy greed, that system which makes a few millionaires and millions of homeless people; that system which defends property and degrades manhood.

At this point a book of political cartoons is placed in my hands, which is a sample of the deception practiced upon the people.

A great street car company is trying to get an extension of its franchise; a large number of people are opposed to granting any more franchises. The Democratic party, through a trick, defeated the people's candidate at the primaries, and now there is no difference between the Democrat or Republican politicians, but they are apparently fighting like Kilkenney cats, and everybody knows it is fair words, deception, and the corporation will get what it wants.

This is only one of the steps that will finally force confiscation of all such property.

"Every bondman and every freeman will cry out for the mountains and rocks to fall upon him and hide him."

This does not say every good man, or every bad man, but everybody.

Mountains and rocks are governments of general and municipal ownership.

Individuality in business will be lost, and the cry will be, "I cannot make a living outside of working for the government." Are we not rapidly preparing the way for these things? Are ye blind that ye cannot see it?

The Sun has entered the sign Aquarius, where there is no star of the first magnitude. While the Sun is here we shall have God's Sunday, and there will be no great men, no privileged class, and no paupers.

On which side will you be found?

Will you be with God and municipal ownership, or will you follishly kick against the pricks and oppose an unconquerable force?

Let me warn ye, rich men, ye had better make your peace with your adversary. Ye can no more stay this move than ye can stop the ocean wave, the winds that blow, or the earth in its revolutions.

Every effort will only make the matter worse when the storm breaks.

Genesis 49-16 says: "Dan shall judge his people, as one of the tribes of Israel." . Verse 17: "Dan shall be a serpent by the way, an adder in the path, that biteth the horse heels, so his rider shall fall backward."

Astrologers figure this sign as the highest and lowest, in its effects, of all of the signs.

In this sign we get the millennium, or equality, of man. A rest from turmoil and strife, just as soon as the workshop is cleansed. Let us cleanse it as quickly as possible.

After the thousand years, Satan is to be loosed for a season to deceive the nations.

How is this?

After the judgment Dan is to bite the horse' heels and cause his rider to fall backwards, i. e., a religious falling away. The horse is the constellation Pegasus, which represents the new system.

I have shown you that Spiritualism is strongest when the Sun is in the air signs, and so strong it is hard to tell the spirits from the people, as they even cohabited. It will be stronger in this sign than it was in the others, in Libra or Gemini.

Let us here caution the Spiritualist to be very careful with whom ye associate. You will do so with people of earth; then how much more careful should you be with those who can make themselves visible or invisible at will? Remember, thoughts are things, and ye have to fight away thoughts, for it is these ye are building into your kingdoms, which will control your next incarnated lives. If ye hold your meetings in the name of God, in the name of Christ, ye will only draw those spirits to you that mean you well.

Let me say to you, church people, do not kick against the pricks; do not oppose Spiritualism, but if you are honest, rather to conduct it in a beneficial way.

I have shown the greatest crime is to go backwards.

In Libra they went back and cohabited with the spirits.

In Gemini, the Garden of Eden, they ate of the forbidden fruit, went back to lust, and were then told to go out and replenish the earth.

The Jews went back to the worship of the golden calf and 4,000 of them lost their lives. Lot's wife only looked back, and it cost her her life.

At the end of the thousand years the lust for power will come upon the people and the terrible competitive systems will again be invoked.

Dan, Aquarius, will cause the rider of the horse to fall backward. This will be a period of second trial, or purgatory.

We now have the most difficult part to explain, and still the most beautiful.

Capricornus starts another week of God's work. It is an earth mental sign, presided over by the great spiritual planet, Saturn, which is called the great evil, who has been let loose in all of his power, and a terrific strife begins between a voluntary justice and the competitive system.

Remember, all that were fit will be taken to a higher sphere, and those who are not will now try to prepare themselves to go higher rather than to enter hades and take another trip around the Zodiac.

Let us see now what Jacob says in the 8th, 9th, 10th, 11th and 12th verses of the 49th chapter of Genesis.

8. "Judah, thou art he whom thy brethren shall praise; thy hand shall be in the neck of thine enemies: thy father's children shall bow down before thee." The whole eleven signs will bow down before Aquarius.

9. "Judah is a lion's whelp; from the prey, my son, thou art gone up: he stooped down, he crouched

as a lion, and as an old lion: who shall rouse him up?"

10. "The sceptre shall not depart from Judah, nor a lawgiver from between his feet, until. Shiloh come; and unto him shall the gathering of the people be."

For the explanation of Shiloh see the solving of the riddle of the Sphinx.

11. "Binding his foal unto the vine, and his ass's colt, unto the choice vine; he washed his garments in wine, and his clothes in the blood of grapes."

12. "His eyes shall be red with wine, and his teeth white with milk."

It is evident, just before the changing of the earth's Poles, our earth will be a very desirable place to live.

Of all the signs, Capricornus will offer the most perfect Monday morning of the whole, while the testing of man's ability of mind over so-called matter, or the higher over the lower, will go on at a high rate.

People born in Capricornus, if they take to politics, are great politicians; they are fine organizers, excellent business people, and are honest more from a sense of duty than a sense of justice.

They are great sticklers for duty. Thus: while the competitive system will be carried on to a great extreme, there will be a form of justice.

Remember, this sign is symbolized by the goat, and Egypt once worshiped the goat, and it is considered one of the most sure-footed, wise and sagacious animals in existence, but very stubborn and tricky.

Remember, also, it was once considered a scapegoat to bear the sins of man.

It is this sign, the closing one before the Sun enters hades, that must bear the brunt of all these changes, and finally reach the salvation of most of those who were not able to graduate before; yet every dainty, luxury and desire of man will be placed before man, but only with natural desires, so that only those who cannot, or will not, overcome must go back over another circuit of the Sun.

Do not fail to read "The Great Prophesy," telling of the time of the setting up of the abomination that maketh desolate.     Price 25c.

What I have written her is testified to in Deuteronomy XXVII-10-11: "Thou shalt therefore obey the voice of the Lord thy God, and do his commandments and his statutes, which I command thee this day."

Everything goes to show, the sin is in going backward. After the long trip of the Sun through the Zodiac, the influence of the signs in going back is terrible.

11. "And Moses charged the people the same day, saying:

12. "These shall stand upon Mount Gerizim to curse the people, when ye are come over Jordan; Simeon, and Levi, and Judah, and Isaachar, and Joseph, and Benjamin."

These signs did not retrograde in civilization.

And these shall stand upon Mount Ebal to curse Reubin, Gad, Asher, Zebulun, Dan and Naphtali. All of these signs retrograded.

Now read the whole chapter, and it will show conclusively that the "forbidden fruit," and great sin is to retrograde in civilization, the thing that will take place at the end of 1,000 years.  It is plain.

THE WHOLE THING IS ASTROLOGICAL.

If you would understand the true meaning of mind and matte you should read the Atomic soul theory

# THE RIDDLE OF THE SPHINX.

**THE SPHINX.**

That there may be no mistake as to what is meant here, I will give a short sketch of the Sphinx as gathered from various works upon the subject.

As there are many structures, pyramids, and forms of the Sphinx which are of much later date than the Pyramid Cheops, and the Sphinx at Gehzeh, it is evident they are mere imitations of the great structures mentioned and were no doubt built for entirely different purposes.  No one can figure how long ago.

Both from a study of the structures themselves and from inscriptions found, it is conceded that the Sphinx was constructed perhaps thousands of years before the Pyramid Cheops was erected; in fact, an

## THE STORY OF THE ZODIAC.

old inscription of Cheops, the builder of the great pyramid, says:

"He has built his pyramid there, where the temple of that goddess (Isis) is, and he has built the pyramid of the Princess Hentsen where that temple is."

Let us here give a description of this gigantic structure. The Encyclopædia Britannica says:

"The Great Sphinx at Gehzeh has the body of a lion crouching close to the ground; the height from the floor or platform on which it lies to the top of the head is 100 feet. The total length is 146 feet; across the shoulders, 34 feet. The head from the top to the chin is 34 feet 6 inches and is calculated to be about 40,000 times the bulk of an ordinary human head. A small temple built between the paws, and the paws, are built of masonry; the balance is carved out of the solid rock. Indeed, it may be safely assumed to be solid, for Colonel Vys drilled a hole 27 feet deep into the shoulder and found so far at least, it was so."

Monetho places the beginning of Egyptian history at 4400 B. C. Even this is disputed by many other searchers after antiquities to prove dates of events of unknown periods.

The Sphinx stands about 9,000 feet east of the pyramids.

There is no doubt that this structure was built to stand as an evidence that a race of men had inhabited the earth who thoroughly understood Astronomy and were far advanced in all branches of science, and that events of time repeat themselves in the course of cycles of time.

There is no doubt that all other structures of this nature were merely imitations of the great Pyramid Cheops.

In regard to the many conjectures as to the purpose of the Sphinx and the mythological story of

THE SPHINX, THE OLDEST RELIC OF ART.

## THE STORY OF THE ZODIAC.

the Greeks, which runs that a fabulous monster which possessed the head of a woman and the body of a lion with wings sat in the highway and every day expounded a riddle to a prominent Theaben, who, failing to solve the riddle, was devoured by the monster, finally the king offered his kingdom and his daughter in marriage to the person who succeeded in solving the riddle. At last one Edipus came from Corinth and when the question was asked, "What animal has a voice and walks on four feet in the morning, two at noon, and three at night?" he replied, "A man, because he creeps on all fours first, then walks on two legs and finally with a cane, making three."

It is said that when the riddle was guessed the monster dropped down and died.

Of course the fact that everybody has wondered what the structure was built for, has suggested that it is a riddle that will some day be solved. There is an ancient prophecy that says the Sphinx will at some period reveal its riddle.

"I am the Sphinx and am in the Desert of Egypt. About my foundations is the sand, and above my head are the stars of heaven. I am the fabled monster of the desert, having the head of Virgo and the body of Leo." Many kings and queens and great men and women have stood before the Sphinx and wondered at the strange silent figure and its riddle. "I am the riddle of the past, and a puzzle to all those who could not expound my riddle or solve my mission. I am the Sphinx, the wonder of the world, and I will break my long silence and give my message to the nations of the earth and to the twelve tribes of Israel."

When the finger of time points into the cycle of Aquarius, then will the Sphinx of the heavens arrive at the Autumnal Equinox.

"I am the Sphinx, the key to time in the heaven,

and thus do I unlock the cycles of time, as I move over the four crosses in the Zodiac.  I am the Shilo of the Hebrew Zodiac, and the key to the Shilo of Jacob and of Joshua, the warrior of time.

"My point in the heavens is between the constillations of Leo and Virgo, and my shape is marked upon certain portions of your earth, as will be revealed when the lost Israel is restored.

"When the stars of the heavens are cast to earth, and the beast with its ten horns and ten crowns rises out of the sea of crystal, then shall my mission be revealed through the intelligence of the Sphinx."

The intelligence of the Sphinx is the arrival of the Sun in the spiritual sign of the Zodiac.  He, the Sun, is not only the Shilo awaited for by Judah, but his arrival in Aquarius shows him to be the lion of Judah, who is to break the seals of the book of Revelations.  He has now arrived in Aquarius, the spiritual part of the celestial head.

See article entitled "Phrenology and the Zodiac; or Man Made in the Likeness and Image of His Creator."

But let us understand something of the RECESSION OF THE EQUINOX.

There are two Zodiacs, or at least two separate divisions; one is the Zodiac or division called the signs, the other is the Zodiac of the constellations.

The Zodiac of the constellations is called "fixed," while the Zodiac of the signs is called "movable."

These once agreed, but at present the signs lie 30 degrees west of the constellations, though the constellations do also move as every atom in nature is movable.

The circle of the Zodiac has a great cross on which the Sun in its great circle moves.

The Sun also has an apparent motion, as it seems to revolve on the cross made by the Winter and

THE STORY OF THE ZODIAC.

THE INTERIOR OR TEMPLE OF THE SPHINX.

## THE STORY OF THE ZODIAC.

Summer Solstices and the Spring and Fall Equinoxes. It is to this crucifixion of the Sun on the cross that all life owes its being.

Were the Sun to perish all life must perish.

I have explained the Zodiac elsewhere as a circle divided into twelve parts called signs, each sign containing 30 degrees. The points of the Equinox have a retrograde motion along the Ecliptic, called "the Recession of the Equinox."

For the last 2,154 years the constellation Pisces has been upon the Vernal Equinox, but the recession of the Equinox has brought the point of the Vernal Equinox into the constellation Aquarius, the water bearer.

There is a question among occult people and students of Astrology as to the time the Sun entered or will enter the constellation at the spring Equinox.

Mr. Butler, in Solar Biology, fixes the date about 250 years ago, while others vary, down to 1899, while the probability is it entered about 70 years ago.

Mr. Charles' Hatfield, in the January number of the Sphinx of 1901, gives the following Bible reason for believing that was the year of the Sun's entrance into Aquarius. He says:

"In order to explain matters, we look to the Astrology of the Scriptures. In chapter IV. of Revelations is a plan of the heavens as follows: The throne in the center is the glorious Sun, the rainbow about the throne is the starry constellations around the heavens. The four and twenty seats are the 24 divisions of the movable Zodiac, or the periods of time of 25,848 years. The four and twenty elders are the constellations as they fill the twenty-four hours of time in the Zodiac. The seven lamps of fire about the throne are the seven heavenly bodies, that were known to the ancients."

(*We now know them as the first octave.*)

## THE STORY OF THE ZODIAC.

"The seven spirits of God denotes the influence of the planets. The sea of glass like unto crystal is the transparent atmosphere from which we draw oxygen or the breath of life.

The four beasts, full of eyes before and behind, are the four constellations, viz: Taurus, the bull; Leo, the lion; Sagittarius, the archer; and Aquila, the eagle. The eyes before and behind are centuries, years, months, weeks, days, hours, minutes, seconds. This denotes time that sees all things that was and is to be. The six wings of each beast denotes the six periods of time, or cycles of time allotted to a quarter of the Zodiac. Each beast represents a period of time, or 6,462, or three times of cycles of 2,154 years.

The Scriptures speak of the four corners of the earth, and it denotes that there are to be four great Empires upon the earth, or the countries that are to become the four great Republics."

*(This will be better understood if you read my book, "What is Coming," price 50c) Stowe.*

"The beast with the face of a lion is Leo, the lion, and has dominion over that part of the earth that is to be under the rule of the nation which has the lion for its emblem, or England.

The beast with the face of a calf is Taurus, and has dominion over that part of the earth under Taurus, or Russia.

As Russia is now in revolution, which will eventually be successful in establishing a republic, they will probably change their emblem and adopt the emblem of the bull, as representing the great agricultural country that it is. (Stowe.)

"The beast with the face of a man is Sagittarius the archer, and has dominion over that part of the earth which is to be ruled by the nation which is to be under Sagittarius, or Spain.

## THE STORY OF THE ZODIAC.

Spain has been cut off for a time for her injustice, but she will regenerate under another speaking tongue, when the period of time is due, and will become a republic.

The fourth beast like a flying eagle is Aquila, the eagle, that lies above Aquarius in the Zodiac. The Eagle has dominion over that part of the earth that is to come under the rule of the nation which has an eagle for its emblem, or the United States."

*I must here drop a lot of irrelevant matter, which rathre weakens than strengthnes Mr. Hatfield's position.*

"The woman in the Scripture with a crown of stars over her head is Columbia, the mother of Freedom. The male child who shall rule the world with a rod of iron represents liberty and freedom, and is influencing the desitny of every true man and woman. I would add that in time, the English-speaking tongue will rule the world, for where that language is used the nations become amalgamated."

*Those who are interested in this should read my book, "What is Coming."*

"The whole world at present appears to be under some exciting and disturbing influence. This influence is affecting empires, countries, and the mental qualities of humanity, because we are coming under a new cycle and a new influence.

For the last 2,154 years we have been under the influence of the constellation of Pisces, a water sign, but the recession of the Equinoxes has brought the Vernal Equinox into the constella of Aquarius, the water bearer."

"The Scripture says there was the noise of a cry from the first fish-gate, and a howling from the second. The second fish-gate was passed during 1899, and the result has been floods, shipwrecks, and many deaths by water, and we will feel the effects for some time to come. During the time of the cycle of Pisces, the waters have been sailed over, and navi-

## THE STORY OF THE ZODIAC.

gation has made great strides and we have developed the powers of the waters, and steam to the utmost extent."

The cry of the first fish-gate was when the Sun entered the sign Pisces and was the great struggle of the Plebians and Patricians of old Rome and other parts of the world, and the howl at the second fish-gate is the struggle of the people against monopoly and the privileged class, taking place at present, and which has been going on since the privileged rottenness that caused the great uprising in France, the American Revolution, and other similar social disturbances of the past 150 years, and is going on today.

"Aquarius, the Vernal Equinox, will bring in the electrical age, and many wonderful inventions and great discoveries will be made, and new powers of the air will become developed; Aquarius will bring about great changes, old things will pass away and new things will be ushered in, for the next cycle of Aquarius of 2,154 years will bring a new religion, and the sixth sense will be developed and become a mental gift to humanity, and we will all be intuitive and magnetic."

*Let the reader remember I have spoken elsewhere of the end of the Pisces world that has taken place. Bible students, not understanding astrology, looked for the destruction of the earth which Ecclesiastes says abideth forever.*

*Let the reader notice what progress is being made with explosives, both in war and peace. Even since I began writing this chapter news comes of wonderful progress in aerial navigation; why?*

*The Vernal Equinox, the Sun or Shilo, has entered an air sign. Though air is a substance and under proper conditions can be seen, so is the spirit of man real and under proper conditions can be seen, and these conditions exist when the Sun is passing*

*through an air sign, and this is why spirit mani-
festation is so much stronger when the Sun has been
or will be in air signs.*

*There is always a physical phenomena accompan-
ies an astronomical phenomena, and these things did
occur, in the early part of the 19th century, like the
shower of falling stars, together with the troublous
times of our own great American Revolution, the
great French Revolution and other uprisings which
closed the 18th century. The Millerites determined
the world must come to an end in July, 1843. They
figured from certain Bible statements, just as Mr.
Hatfield has done.*

*"Following the Millerite excitement of 1843 came
the inittiation of Spiritualism by the Fox sisters in
1848, and shortly after the discovery of nitro-glycer-
ine and the increased use of gas, alcohol and other
explosives, in mechanical work, this would lead us
to suppose the Sun had already crossed the line into
Aquarius. As Uranus is to commence his rule, and
the fall of the money power take place amid great
confusion, and that has not taken place, we must
suppose the Sun entered Aquarius since Uranus was
last in his own house, hence the Sun probably entered Aquarius about 70 years ago.*

*"As Uranus, will enter his house in 1912, we may
look for great excitement and the overthrow of the
present money worshiping system, within the next
few years. It would be wise for those living in the
big cities to seek homes in quiet country places before that time.*

*"The poles of Equinox retrograde along the Eclip-
tic about 2½ seconds of a degree per year. The
points of the Equinox make a recession of one degree in 71⅔ years, or one whole sign in 26,154 years.*
*"In the Scriptures the constellation of Pisces ends
with the times of the gentiles."*

## THE STORY OF THE ZODIAC.

These began when Nebuchadnezzar assumed the crown of Babylon. His accession took place in the year 3377 A. M. The "Times of the Gentiles" ended 2,520 years after, or in March of 5897 A. M., or the spring of 1899 A. D., when Aquarius was at the Vernal Equinox.

According to some astrologers' calculations, it gave Sunday, Feb. 12th, 1899, as the period for the cycle of Aquarius to begin.

*I cannot accept this, as it is not likely the period would begin until Uranus is in his own house, which will not. occur until October, 1912. However, he began his influence at the date given, 1899, as he had then left the orbes of the influence of the water sign Scorpio, and Saturn had passed beyond orbes of conjunction with him, while Jupiter was passing out of the air sign Libra. Heliocentrically.*

"When Leo was at the Vernal Equinox, about 12,944 years ago, the Egyptians probably carved the sphinx, Virgo and Leo, as represented by the body of a lion and the face of a woman."

"At the time the constellation Argo Navis was at the Vernal Equinox, the flood occurred, and when the Star 'Nods' in the oar-lock of the ship, was on a line with the Equinox, Noah entered the Ark."

The reason of using this lengthy quotation, is that Brother Hatfield has given the matter much study, though it is claimed he borrowed many of his ideas from. Prof. Henry, of Boston. Be this as it may, I cannot fully agree with the figures given. He. seems to think the sinking of Atlantis came with the flood of Noah, but Atlantis was undoubtedly of a period much earlier and of a far greater flood, as I have explained before.

He says: "About 16,078 years ago, when the scientific constellation Virgo was at the Vernal Equinox, there must have been a great civilization on the earth, and when Leo was at the Vernal Equinox the

## THE STORY OF THE ZODIAC.

astrologers foresaw that some great calamity would overtake the world by water. Then comes the period of Noah."

While this is in the main true, the Noah flood came at a much later period. Besides, he does not seem to understand the air signs are productive of far more good than the fire, earth or water signs. The latter being the cold, selfish signs. He says:

"The point of the Vernal Equinox is truly the finger of time, and it signifies what has been and what is to be."

A very ancient Zodiac and that of Denderah placed Leo at the head of the Zodiac, and Dupius calculated the Sphinx was carved over 15,000 years ago. But, we started our period over 20,000 years ago when the Sun was in the sign Capricornus.

In recent excavations on the site of old Babylon earthen tablets were found showing the great flood occurred when the Sun was in Capricornus; this does not mean that a flood did not take place when the Sun was at its northern position, but the flood was the greater flood when the Sun was going out of Capricornus. Yet it was a terrible flood that destroyed the wonderful civilization of the Noah period. The southern flood will again destroy the great civilization of the world in about 4,000 years.

Some believe, because of certain astronomical positions, the destruction will be by fire instead of water, and that not until the Sun has entered Sagittarius.

In the following cut I am supposed to reveal the riddle of the Sphinx.

Let the reader observe the figures in each sign of the Zodiac is only to give the approximate time the Sun is in each sign in transiting the circle, whether he takes 25,000 years, more or less, according to different authors, I do not care to discuss here, but taking Jacob's blessing of Judah for a text, where he

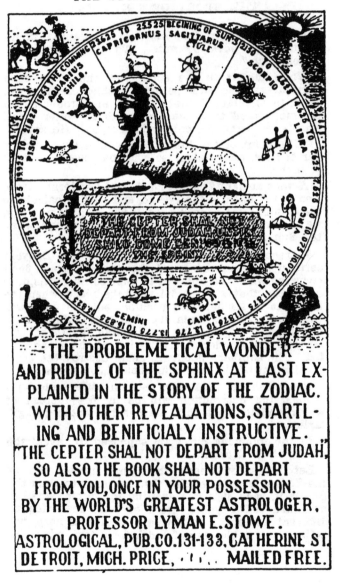

THE PROBLEMETICAL WONDER
AND RIDDLE OF THE SPHINX AT LAST EX-
PLAINED IN THE STORY OF THE ZODIAC.
WITH OTHER REVEALATIONS, STARTL-
ING AND BENIFICIALY INSTRUCTIVE.
"THE CEPTER SHAL NOT DEPART FROM JUDAH,"
SO ALSO THE BOOK SHAL NOT DEPART
FROM YOU, ONCE IN YOUR POSSESSION.
BY THE WORLD'S GREATEST ASTROLOGER,
PROFESSOR LYMAN E. STOWE.
ASTROLOGICAL, PUB. CO. 131-133, CATHERINE ST.
DETROIT, MICH. PRICE, ..... MAILED FREE.

says, Genesis 49:10: "The sceptre shall not depart
from Judah (Capricornus) or a law giver from between his feet, until Shiloh come; and unto him
shall the gathering of the people be." Which evidently means, a spiritual guidance, has been and will
be with man until Shiloh, the Vernal Equinox, or the
Sun shall reach that point again.

I have shown the growth of vegetation brought
the sleeping soul atoms from earth to life
and then this life gradually evolved through
insect and animal life to man, and that sex
worship recognized evolution and re-incarnation,
hence the erection of the Sphinx at that period of
great civilization, as a standing evidence to man,
that man and beast are of the one origin, evolving
from vegetation and insect life into beast, and lastly
man; he reached the zenith of his beastly power
when the Sun reached Leo, and man sacrificed so
many of his kind to his superstitions.

Civilization relapsed and the beast power revived
when the Sun passed through Taurus and Aries; and
man persecuted his kind for selfish gains, while the
Sun is in Pisces or for the past two thousand years.
Now the Sun has entered Aquarius, the type of the
Celestial head or the spiritual sign, or the sign of
the man or water bearer. Baptismo, where justice,
equality, human liberties, even to recognizing of the
rights of the brute, take place; but why the female
head? Why not the male head?

It is through the female as well as the male the
evolution out of hades has been possible, and woman
must have her equal rights with man, and it is only
since the Sun has entered Aquarius she has asserted
her rights and is beginning to get them, hence the
Sphinx riddle is revealed, the seals of the book of
Revelation broken by the lion of Judah or Sun entering the sign Aquarius. The Sun in the lion of Judah
because he represents Joseph or Leo. He has advanced through the signs until he has entered the

### THE STORY OF THE ZODIAC.

sign Aquarius, ruled by Uranus, his only begotten son.

Let not the superstitious and the bigot be frightened and think I am trying to rob his Christ of his glory, for whether there ever was such a being or not, or whether he comes again or not, here are astrological and astronomical truths, backed by the works of ancient man, which he can use as a testimony of his way of thinking. I do not pretend to say which way it is; I merely give reason backed up by facts.

The very wise men, astronomers and college professors, may pooh-pooh at this work, because I am not of them, i. e., did not receive the stamp of a college education. But as Matthew xi:25 says: "God takes the small things of earth to confound the wise," or "Thou hast hidden these things from the wise and prudent, and hast revealed them unto babes."

It is possible for a true searcher for knowledge to learn the movements of the planets and other great truths outside of college. Even Mother Shipton, whose prophesies were made so long ago and so many of them came true, says:

All England's sons that plow the land
Shall be seen with book in hand.
Learning shall so ebb and flow
The poor shall most wisdom know.
The world to an end shall come
In eighteen hundred and eighty-one.

It is a fact that will be recognized that wise men are sometimes re-incarnated, as a testimony or to reveal certain knowledge, as was Elijah, and though their knowledge is of a former life, like the natural mathematician or musical prodigy, they cannot tell from whence it comes.

As for myself, I make no claims, but I have often

been astonished at my own predictions and wondered from whence came my knowledge, which I find is generally correct.

I wish the reader to understand I am not opposed to wealth getting or to wealthy men, but I am opposed to a privileged class using unjust powers to rob others, or, in a humbler term, I am opposed to one animal, because of his hoggishness, getting into the trough and spoiling tne swill which is in abundance for the whole herd. The heads of corporations and trusts are worse than swine.

Man is a selfish being, and some men to be able to lord it over others, and for fear they will not get their share, create false laws and false systems to keep others down, hence God will soon furnish us a system that will force all men to become equal before and to recognize the rights of the dumb brute. It is here that man must recognize the hand of God, the truth, the laws, of evolution and re-incarnation. He must recognize that every heavenly body is a great living, thinking being; that there are worlds and worlds within worlds; that man in the process of evolution is in God's workshop. Thus there could be no such place as heaven, as the grandest heaven would grow monotonous and become a hell; man can only enjoy more because he knows more; he can only know more through experience. A simple belief cannot save man. Finally we have reached the millenium or God's Sunday, a period of rest or equality of mankind, before the law, and the rights of the brute must be recognized. Then comes the graduation day and another one of God's weeks of work.

This is the riddle of the Sphinx.

The breaking of the seals of Revelations by the Sun's arrival in Aquarius; he is the Lion of the 12 tribes of Judah, or 12 signs of the Zodiac.

# THE NEW TESTIMENT IN ASTROLOGY.

Religious people, who have heretofore opposed astrology on religious grounds, to be consistent, must admit the Bible an allegory based on astrology or else admit astrology is a testimony of the truth of the Bible and basis of all religion.

## THE NEW TESTAMENT IN ASTROLOGY.

If it was necessary to frequently look at the illustration of the Zodiac in reading the Astrological story of the Old Testament, it is doubly so in reading the story of the New Testament.

But before we proceed let us go back to the introductory pages of this article, where I have referred to the circle, half circle and the cross, all taken from astrology.

The ancient astrologers saw that everything in nature moves in circles of time, coming back to the same events after great lapse of time, hence the circle was adopted as the symbol of the Sun, the life-giver, and as the symbol of eternal life.

The Mohammedans are fatalists, hence believe man came on the earth for experience. They believ God himself could never know the difference between pain and pleasure, if he never thought of the two opposites.

Believing God is in everything, they believe there is no room for anything else but God, and man, being a part of God, he is fated to just what he does do. Hence, all that came to this earth came for ex-

## THE STORY OF THE ZODIAC.

perience, that they may go back to enjoy more because the know more. But as they believe this earth is God's workshop, they believe the spirit state is a place of rest, hence to them the Sun means eternal life, and the Moon, the spirit state or only state of rest, while the cross in the circle is a symbol of life on earth, or body and labor. Ancient astrology was, of course, the basis of this belief.

# THE TWELVE SIGNS OF THE ZODIAC

With all of this they believe man has a certain amount of free moral agency. They also believe in reincarnation, hence the harder man strives to obey the promptings of the God within, he will rest the happier and longer in the spirit state and finally go to a higher sphere.

## THE STORY OF THE ZODIAC.

I have no quarrel with the beautiful allegorical character of Christ, and prefer to believe it is one phase of the great plan of God, as Astrology is another, and a greater testimony of God's great plan.

It is more rational to me than a story that tells me GOD SAYS I MUST LOVE MY ENEMIES WHILE HE ROASTS HIS.

While I shall attempt to show that the story of the Christian religion is enacted by the Sun and stars, every year as a testimony of the truth of the Christian religion, I have not hesitated to give the other side of the question.

The Astrological symbol of the Earth is a circle with the cross inside of the circle.

Where did the first idea of the cross come from?

Notice the principal cut, which should have ben elliptic in shape, the long part from top to bottom, or north and south. This represents the winter and summer solstice or the long part of the cross.

Now we will notice from east to west we have the equator or spring and fall equinox, when the days and nights are of the same length.

We now observe the Sun is crucified on this cross. Born on the upper end of the cross in December, passes to the spring equinox, March 21st. He now moves on to June 21st, the Summer Stolstice, where the days begin to shorten.

This is John the Baptist, born six months before the Sun God. It says in John III-30: "He must increase, but I must decrease." There can be no other meaning put to this than a reference to the day's length. The Sun now moves to the fall equinox. He has now passed over three-fourths of his cross; in other words, he has his cross on his back, "bearing his cross to his crucifixion," Just as Christ did. The two heavenly thieves are November and December, the only months in the year in which there is no harvest of consequence on the face of the globe.

## THE STAR OF BETHLEHEM.

VENUS—LOVE

Speculation has supposed many stars to be the star of the east. A conjunction of Jupiter and other stars, comets, the mighty Sirius and others. But Venus, the Goodess of Love, fills the bill in every particular, including LUCIFER, thelight bearer, and Judas, the traitor.

VENUE, the GODDESS OF LOVE, OR LUCIFER, the LIGHT BEARER, generally morning star in the spring and summer months; in the fall the tip of the earth makes it appear to change its position and become evening star, and lead on a heavenly host, seemingly crowding the sun back. This gave rise to the passage in Isaiah xiv., 12: "How art thou fallen from heaven, O! Lucifer, son of the morning?"

No doubt this star also became the Judas Iscariot who betrayed the son of God, or the sun god.

The following is a quotation from Webster's dictionary, in reference to the word Lucifer:

"The application of this passage, in Isaiah, to Satan and to the fall of the apostate angels, is one of those gross perversions of sacred writ which so extensively obtain, and which are to be traced to a proneness to seek for more in a given passage than it contains— a disposition to be influenced by sound rather than by sense, and an implicit faith in revealed interpretations.—Henderson."

We believe a study of the stars opens the most direct road to the understanding of God's plan, and that there is much truth mixed with fiction and allegory in the old stories of mythology, and the study of these stories from an astrological standpoint will prove beneficial to the student.

There is a strong resemblance in this comparison of the SON of God and Sun God to the many stories in mythology based upon the heavenly bodies. See sketches in Stowe's Astrological Periodicity.

## THE STORY OF THE ZODIAC.

Let me here speak of the star of Bethlehem, which the wise men saw led to the stable where the Son of God or the Sun God was born.

We are assessed for our taxes in the spring and pay them in the fall. Our laws are based upon those of the ancients. Besides, man pays his taxes after harvesting his summer work. Well, the Jews went up to Jerusalem to be taxed, and this was in the spring of the year, when it was still cold and the inns full, and the people complained but the wise men, AND ASTROLOGERS WERE ALWAYS CALLED WISE MEN, encouraged the people by pointing out the star that foretold the birth of the Sun God, they knew was born in the stable, between the horse and the goat.

Because the inns were overcrowded, the people suffered and complained.

The days were beginning to lengthen, the Sun to grow stronger, warming the earth, bringing up the young shoots and preparing the ground for plowing, thus coming to the salvation of man.

This star is always found in the east as morning star, and this is no doubt the star of Bethlehem.

We call it Venus, the Goddess of Love. They called it Lucipher, the light-bearer.

We shall find this same star playing the part of Judas Iscariot, the betrayer.

Acts I-18 says: "And this man purchased a field with the reward of iniquity, and falling headlong, he burst asunder in the midst, and all his bowels gushed out."

And Matt. XXVII-5 says: "And he cast down the pieces of silver in the temple and departed, and went and hanged himself." (Contradictory.)

This, with the evidence cited on pages 31 and 32 of this book, makes one hesitate any say, "Well, the whole Bible looks like an allegory," but if an allegory, it is an allegory of stupendous truth, and there can be no harm in believing the story true; but do not

## THE STORY OF THE ZODIAC.

let us hesitate in our research. We know history points to twenty-one Saviors and many Bibles. We cannot help but ask ourselves, which is the right one, or are they all allegories of the one and the same stupendous plan of God?

There are many religions and many divisions or denominations of each religion.

Which is right?

Astrology is the basis of all, and it proves itself, and is true. Even the followers of the Christian religion do not agree, much less practice, what they preach.

### THE THREE WISE MEN (ASTROLOGERS).

Pointing out Venus, the morning star, in the east, which heralds the rebirth of the Sun. Good old summer time—plenty to eat again.

The story of the Son of God, and the story of the Sun God—a myth or a parallel, which is it?

## THE STORY OF THE ZODIAC.

### WE WILL NOW TAKE UP THE STORY OF THE

### SON OF GOD AND THE STORY

### OF THE SUN GOD.

Here I insert a cut and ask the reader to remember IN THE STORY OF THE OLD TESTAMENT we started with the line of Capricornus and Sagittarius and went down to the right through Libra, as this is the real course of the Sun in the great Zodiac. Now we commence at the same point and go to the left, through Aquariu.., Pisces and Aries, and so around the Zodiac, as this is the apparent annual course of the Sun caused by the revolutions of the Earth.

Every time we speak of the Sun's movements from one sign to another, let us go back and look at the illustration, and the story can be more easily understood.

No intelligent man will deny the character of Christ is an ideal character. But is it a child of fancy, or was there a real character called Christ, a Nazarene, the son of Mary and God Almigthy?

We know historians who are contemporaneous and write of things of their own times can hardly ever tell the truth. Then how can we look for truth when historians write of things a hundred and fifty years before their time?

It has been admitted, even by Christian theologians, that not a book of the New Testament was ever written until 150 years after the supposed birth of Christ.

Who are the historians that wrote the New Testament. Certainly not Mathew, Mark, Luke and John, because these books say, "According to Matthew," "According to Luke," etc., etc., etc. No writer would say according to so and so, but I say so. Very well; if they did not write the books, who did? Why, the priests of that time, of course.

## THE STORY OF THE ZODIAC.

Back as far as ancient Egypt the priests were supposed to be the only class of beings who were wise, and were so called the wise men. Most of them were Astrologers, until other people began to study Astrology. Then the priests abused Astrology and substituted secret forms and unknown tongues to deceive the people.

Says Zell's Encyclopedia: "As soon as authentic traditions of the origin of the universe was lost or adulterated by the inventions of men, then fable and fiction began to prevail."

"The priesthood monopolized all of the religion, and all of the learning, as well as all arts and science. In order, therefore, to keep the laity in subjection, besides preventing all individual improvement, they performed all of the ministrations of religion in unknown tongues and covered them with a thick veil of fable and allegory."

It is left for me to prove that the present Christian religion is but an allegory of ancient Sun worship, or rather based on Astrology.

It is true that great religious upheavals and excitements occur at stated periods, especially every six hundred years.

But the story of the Son of God and the story of the Sun God are one and the same story.

In a book I am about to publish, entitled "The Spiritual Side of Astrology," I seek to make plain Astrology is the basis of all religion, Mythology and Free Masonry. Here I wish to show the story of the Christian religion is being enacted by the Sun and stars every year.

Now let us look at the accompanying cut and follow the parallel of the stories.

The Son of God was born, we say, the 25th day of December. He was his own father and he was born in a stable.

# THE TWELVE SIGNS OF THE ZODIAC

## SEE CUT.

Now the Sun is re-born every year on the 25th day of December; that is, the days begin to lengthen. It is the winter solstice. He is his own father. He is born in the stable between the constellations of the horse and goat, Sagittarius and Capricornus.

The Bible uses a day for a year. The Astrologer uses a day for a year.

Thirty years after Christ's birth he was baptized. Thirty days after the Sun is born he enters the sign

## THE STORY OF THE ZODIAC.

Aquarius, the water-bearer (Baptismo). After his baptism Christ took his disciples from among the fishermen, and the Sun next enters the sign Pisces, the fishes. We observe Lent and eat fish one day of the week in honor of the Sun's passage through the sign of the fishes.

Look at the cut again. Christ then became the good shepherd of the flock. The Sun enters the sign Aries, the lamb. He is yet young, the lamb or the young Sun God.

Christ then went out to the salvation of men. Let us see how the Sun God goes out to the salvation of men.

The ancients had consumed the products of the year before and were praying for their Sun God to come back and warm the earth, to bring forth vegetation, which all animal life required. He came, and now he must go forth to the salvation of man; fit the fields for plowing. The bull comes in here for his share of glory, and he is worshiped, because he represents agriculture. The fields are plowed and seed is sown for a late harvest. Look at the cut—the twins represent increase.

Christ spoke of the backsliders. Every year the Sun enters the sign Cancer, June 21st to July 22d, symbolized by the crab, which crawls backward, and all vegetation dries up and retreats back into the earth.

This is the summer solstice, or John the Baptist, born just six months before Christ, and who says, John III-30, "He must increase and I must decrease."

Christ became the Lion of the twelve tribes of Judah. Every year the Sun enters the sign Leo, the lion, and becomes the Lion of the Twelve Signs of the Zodiac.

When? Why, the 22d of July to 23d of August, when the Sun is hottest; exerts most power, the "Lion."

## THE STORY OF THE ZODIAC.

Let the reader look at the cut at each paragraph or description of each sign.

Our Christian friends sup to the vestal virgin. When? Every year when the Sun enters the sign Virgo, whose symbol is the Virgin, August 23d to September 23d. Now look at the cut and the central cross, on which the Sun is Crucified every year, and you will see the Sun has passed over the cross on which he is annually crucified. and, like Christ, has his cross on his back—i. e., passed over it.

Our Christian friends lay much stress upon the judgment day. Every year, on the 23d day of September, the Sun enters the sign Libra, symbolized by the balance. Every year after harvest the farmer balances up his books and pays his debts. But there the Sun God presents a parallel to the Son of God on the road to the crucifixion. The Sun begins to retreat, the days to grow shorter. The Sun, like Christ, is bearing his cross toward the crucifixion. Keep the eye on the cut. The Son of God was crucified between the two thieves. The Sun God is crucified between the two heavenly thieves, Scorpio and Sagittarius, October 23d to November 22d—November 22d to December 21st. There is a harvest somewhere every month in the year, except these two months, the heavenly thieves.

The Sun lost its power, retreated back where it is white and cold. But Sagittarius became the repentant thief, gives up, does not wait until January 1st, but gives up December 25th. And after the Sun comes out of hades, where he was for three days, while the days are of one length, he is re-born, the same as Christ. There are three days about the same length, the three days the Son of God was supposed to have descended into hades.

Is this not complete?

Have I left anything out?
What? You say No?

Yes, I have left out the betrayer.

## THE STORY OF THE ZODIAC.

Who was the betrayer?

Judas Iscariot was Christ's betrayer.

But who was the Sun God's betrayer?

The ancients had noticed, notwithstanding their prayers and sacrifices, every year the Sun deserted them and went back until, to them, he died, was finally resurrected. They could not believe their loved Sun God could willingly desert them, so they looked into the heavens to see why he went back.

In the fall, every year, they saw him retreat, apparently followed by a tremendous heavenly host, for there are more stars in the constellations Libra, Scorpio and Sagittarius than in any others, and it was these stars that seemed to be chasing and pressing the Sun back. They were led on by a bright and beautiful star the ancients had seen in the east, in early morning, in spring and summer months, just as we do now. By the tip of the earth he has apparently fallen to evening star, leading on the heavenly host. We call it Venus, the Goddess of Love. They called it "Lucifer, the light-bearer."

So they cried, "How art thou fallen fro heaven, O Lucifer, Star of the Morning?" And so here you have the story of the war in heaven.

## THE KISS OF BETRAYAL.

Let me here call attention to another phase of the story, though bearing more heavily in favor of the ideal than the real. I am compelled to give the Catholic Church a considerable credit here, for holding in form at least the sacredness of virtue which they hold to so strongly in the celibacy of the priesthood and sacredness of the marriage ties, if not in the immaculate conception. All of this was no doubt drawn from a parallel story in the heavens, originally by the sex worshippers.

Christ, the Son of God, was always talking out of doors, mostly in the summer time. So do we look upon the sun, mostly in summer

Christ had 12 disciples.

## THE STORY OF THE ZODIAC.

The sun has 12 disciples or 12 signs of the Zodiac.

Christ was betrayed by a kiss from Judas Iscariot.

The sun is betrayed by a kiss from Lucifer, the light bearer, we call Venus the Goddess of Love.

Christ was wont to go to the garden of Gethsemane, where he was finally pursued by the hosts, led on by Judas Iscariot.

Where this garden was situated no one knows.

The word Gethsemane means olives or oil press— says Potter.

The sun takes his course through the gardens of the summer months, pursued by the heavenly host of stars of Sagittarius, the sign of religion, and Scorpio and Libra, led on by Lucifer, the light bearer, or Venus.

As Judas betrayed Christ, so does Lucifer or Venus betray the sun in this way.

The sun is the life giver, yet stands alone in his virtue.

Knowing his time has come to be crucified, he offers the last supper of the harvest year, after which he offers a sop to the 12 signs or disciples; that is, in the fall as in the spring there is apparently a new lease of life, animal desires are strengthened as if for a temptation for self destruction. Old age forgets its weakness and wastes vital forces. The lower animals propagate their species; even the trees and flowers put forth new efforts. This is the sop the sun gives at the last supper.

Venus, the Goddess of Love, or Lucifer, as they called it, exerts the influences of passion on all nature, the kiss of betrayal, that is, the wages of sin is death. The old man loses his vitality, the lower animals bring forth their young to perish by the rigors of winter, the trees and flowers are caught by the early frosts; thus, "The wages of sin is death." All the results of the betrayal by a kiss of passion,

## THE STORY OF THE ZODIAC.

for which Lucifer, i. e., Venus, the Goddess of Love, is ashamed of.

We must remember that Judas betrayed the Master for 30 pieces of silver. Matthew xxvii:5 says:

"And he cast down the pieces of silver in the temple, and went out and hanged himself."

Here the writer evidently made a mistake. There was no parallel for his hanging himself, but a later writer seeing the error, astrologically says—Acts 1:18:

"Now this man purchased a field with the reward of iniquity; and falling headlong, he burst asunder in the midst, and all his bowels gushed out." (See cut of cosmic man.)

## THE COSMIC MAN.

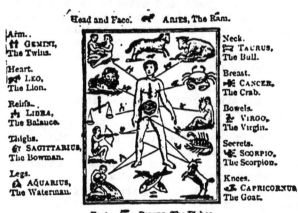

Head and Face. ♈ ARIES, The Ram.

Arm.
♊ GEMINI, The Twins.

Heart.
♌ LEO, The Lion.

Reins.
♎ LIBRA, The Balance.

Thighs.
♐ SAGITTARIUS, The Bowman.

Legs.
♒ AQUARIUS, The Waterman.

Neck.
♉ TAURUS, The Bull.

Breast.
♋ CANCER, The Crab.

Bowels.
♍ VIRGO, The Virgin.

Secrets.
♏ SCORPIO, The Scorpion.

Knees.
♑ CAPRICORNUS, The Goat.

Feet. ♓ PISCES, The Fishes.

We must remember that at the time Christ was betrayed it was in the garden at night time.

The silver moon is the ruler of the night, and the beautiful autumn nights are longer than the days,

## THE STORY OF THE ZODIAC.

and there are 30 degrees in each sign. These 30 silver moon nights are the 30 pieces of silver Lucifer, Venus, betrayed the sun for. He had been the morning star, but now betrayed for the 30 pieces of silver night, but now cast them down in the potter's field a graveyard of fall tragedies and disappears here, only to appear again as morning star in the spring, and we see nothing but the man with his bowels broke asunder, which covers Virgo, Libra and Scorpio to the secrets, and Lucifer disappears, to be born again in the springtime.

We must remember a piece of silver was of but 13 cents of our money or 30 pieces of but $3.90; a very small sum to get for the betrayal to death.

That is an evidence of an allegory.

Which is it, a sacred novel founded on astronomy, or is the story of the Son of God paralleled in the heavens as a testimony?

The truths supposed to be spoken by Christ stamp the character too grand and noble to be cast down, whichever way it is, and if I must err I will err on the side that bears the strongest testimony. If I accept it as an allegory I have but one side; if I accept it as a parallel I have a testimony.

Now which is it?

Is the Christian religion, with all other religions, together with Mythology and Free Masonry, based upon Astrology? Or is it a fact that the Sun and stars are enacting the story of the Christian religion every year? Is the fact about to be recognized that the observation of Sunday as a religious holiday originated with an Astrologer, and is a testimony that the whole work is Astrological?

Is Astrology the rejected corner-stone about to be acknowledged again?

In either case, our Christian friends should honor the Astrologer for unearthing the truth, and showing Astrology is the road to truth and the salvation of man.

## THE STORY OF THE ZODIAC.

I have just been asked, is there nothing different, in exact wording, to denote Astrology in the Bible?

I answer, Yes.

I have already given enough, but I will go farther and call the attention to the frequent use of the numbers 7 and 12 and their frequent use in the Bible and in Astrology.

Note, for ages there were counted but 7 heavenly bodies in our solar system, including the Sun and Moon, though the others were undoubtedly known to the ancient Astrologers.   There are 12 signs of the Zodiac, and the 360 degrees of the Zodiac are divisable by 12 without a remainder; besides, these numbers are most frequently used in the Bible.

Remember, there were 7 days of the week, named after the 7 bodies of our Solar system.   I could fill pages of the frequent Biblical use of the number 7.

*Book of Judges*

Judges V-18 says: "Zebulun and Naphtali were a people who jeoparded their lives unto the death, in the high places of the field."

Now remember what I have said of the signs Cancer and Pisces.  The ages ruled by these signs are periods of gathering wealth, regardless of the rights and sufferings of man, and Christ says "It is easier for a camel to pass through the needle's eye than for a rich man to enter the kingdom of heaven."

In the 20th verse it says:  "They fought from heaven, the stars in their courses fought against Sisera."

21.  "The river of Kishon swept them away."

That this is Astrological, there is not a shadow of doubt, as there is not, nor ever was, a river called Kishon.

Fanatics who have cut out over 20 books from the Bible and innumerable passages, to make it appear to support their particular dogmas, have tried to account for the mighty river of time by pretending to find a little, short, sluggish stream, called Mukutta, is the mighty river of time referred to.  This little

### THE STORY OF THE ZODIAC.

stream runs through  amarsh and empties into the Bay of Acre, says Potter's Bible Encyclopedia.

But this passage distinctly states, the stars in their courses fought, and they do and will fight, changing these various conditions, as the Sun in its great Zodiac passes from one sig¹n to another.

In the original text of Genesis I-14 it reads: "Let there be light, to divide the day from the night, and let them be for SIGNS and for SEASONS, and for NATIONS."

Why have these last six words been left out of modern Bibles?

The answer is clear. Crazy fanatics who were prejudiced against what they could not understand, have mutilated the Bible to make it fit their dogmas, until they have made the most of it a conglomerate, inconsistent mass, which they cannot consistently explain; but Astrology makes all plain.

Elsewhere in this work I have brought indisputable evidence that the Bible was written for a guide of justice for LABOR UNIONS, which were finally taken possession of by political tricksters and degenerated into a society called Free Masons. This enraged the honest laborers, who were too poor to become Masons, and the priesthood sought to organize them into followers and supporters of their dogmas. Some of these had honest intentions, while others used their knowledge of Astrology to build a theology to increase their following, and so to quiet the laborers' demands for justice they have been promised a reward of mansions in the skies and eternal rest and happiness in a mythical heaven.

But the stars in the skies fight against this and will bring order out of chaos.

Now look at Ecclesiastes III-1 to 8.

1. "To every thing there is a season, and a time to every purpose under the heaven.

2. "A time to be born, and a time to die; a time to plant, and a time to pluck up that which is planted.

## THE STORY OF THE ZODIAC.

3. "A time to kill, and a time to heal; a time to break down, and a time to build up.

4. "A time to weep, and a time to laugh; a time to mourn, and a time to dance.

5. "A time to cast away stones, and a time to gather stones together; a time to embrace, and a time to refrain from embracing.

6. "A time to get, and a time to lose; a time to keep, and a time to cast away.

7. "A time to rend, and a time to sew; a time to keep silent, and a time to speak.

8. "A time to love, and a time to hate; a time of war, and a time of peace."

This writer was an Astrologer. If every man understood Astrology, he would know when he is likely to meet with misfortune, and so to keep still or avoid the rending, and thus avoid the mending.

In my Astrological Periodicity I show any man how to know the most of his good and evil periods, so he may take advantage of them, and by noting his periods of the past, if they are correct, he cannot help admitting the truth of those of the future.

There never was a book writen that gives so much value for $2.00 as this wonderful guide to doctors, officers of the law, or all kinds of professional men, business men and farmers, as well as to the masses of the people. It is the result of many years of hard labor.

Who would not take advantage of the knowledge which would benefit him, if he knew it?

The commercial reports claim that 95 per cent of all business men fail, sooner or later, and I will wager I can tell any man the years which his misfortune came upon him, or the years of the greatest evils of his life, as soon as I get his date of birth. Anyone sending me his place and date of birth, including the hour, if possible, with his address and $1.00 to pay my typewriter and other expenses, I will give him his characteristics, nature, what local-

## THE STORY OF THE ZODIAC.

ity and occupation will be best for him, together with his good and evil periods. Shakespeare says:

"There is a tide in the affairs of man which, if taken at its flood, leads on to fortune."

Then why not take advantage of it?

After reading the above you will naturally ask why do I not take advantage of it, and I will to the best of my ability. But I did not know. Had I known of Astrology what I know now, and what you can know, I would be in much better shape than I now am in.

--

## THE NEW JERUSALEM.

**Though the Whole Bible Is the Story of the Zodiac, the New Testament Is Particularly So.**

The Books of Daniel and Revelations are two more distinctly astrological works than any others, and as these books refer almost exclusively to the closing drama of the Pisces cycle and the opening of the Aquarius cycle, it is best not to go into the matter here, especially as I have already gone over these two books throroughly, in my book "What Is Coming." It is not my purpose to have much to say of them here only so far as the reference to astrological terms and the reference to the Zodiac is forcefully manifest.

There are several references to the New Jerusalem, which evidently refer to the new Zodiac or the sun passing through Aquarius.

It is very clearly evident the astrologers were so bitterly opposed by the priesthood, who were generally in league with the kings and politicians, that they were compelled to write under symbols. Knowing the wise men of the future would know how to interpret the symbols, and it is very amusing to note where the priesthood, ignorant of the great science, have added their false and silly doctrines to the work, not knowing such interpretations could be easily detected.

According to chapter XXI of Revelations, this new Jerusalem is to be as big one way as the other, as high as it is broad.

Chapter XI says, "And there was given me a reed like a rod; and the angel stood, saying, 'Rise, and measure the temple of God, and the altar, and them that worship therein."

## THE STORY OF THE ZODIAC.

"But the court which is without the temple leave out and measure it not; for it is given unto the gentiles; and the holy city shall they tread under foot forty and two months."

Notice the Zodiac has an east, west, north and south side, with three gates or angles on each side.

The temple referred to the Zodiac in general, while the New Jerusalem refers only to the new conditions of things after social conditions have settled down from the great social upheaval about to take place caused by the changed conditions the sun's entrance into Aquarius will produce.

The Zodiac being a band eight to nine degrees each side of the ecliptic, the space outside of that was referred to as the court, not expected to be measured.

The third verse of the XI chapter of Revelations says, "And I will give power to my two witnesses, and they shall prophesy a thousand, two hundred and three score days clothed in sackcloth."

Let us note who these two witnesses are. They are the two systems of astrology: the Helio system recognizing the sun as the center, and the Geo system recognizing the earth as the center.

I will show that twelve is a prophetic number.

There were twelve sons of Ishmael, that represented twelve princes or twelve cities.

There were twelve sons of Jacob, representing twelve tribes of Judah.

There were twelve apostles.

There are twelve signs of the Zodiac.

The Zodiac has been used for all time as a basis for the measurement of the heavens. This is divided into twelve parts of thirty degrees, or it is subdivided into degrees, minutes and seconds.

For many ages 360 days constituted a year, but as this system was forever a worry because of the running of the seasons over and into each other, hence

## THE STORY OF THE ZODIAC.

a more scientific form had to be adopted.  This was first attempted by Julius Caesar, who employed two Chaldean mathematicians (46 B. C.) to make the calculations.  This was afterward corrected several times, until the Gregory system was finally adopted in 1582.

The clock dial and the Zodiac are in the same form of dviision.

The Bible tells you to use a day for a year.  A time spoken of in Daniel 7:25—12:7, and in Revelation 12:6-14.  A time is 360 days, or 1 year.  Times 720, a half a time 180; this makes 1,260 years so often referred to as a prophetic period.  Thus these witnesses were to prophesy in sackcloth one thousand two hundred and threescore years, or 1,260 years, and it has been just about that length of time since astrology was driven under cover by the priesthood, and there must still be a struggle before the matter is settled, but according to this prophecy, whatsoever is done unto them will be meted out in full to their persecutors.

The New Jerusalem is to bring about a new order of things, so grandly glorious in comparison to past ages that the most magnificent and extravagant descriptive matter was used in describing this wonderful change where such heavenly conditions are to exist that God is said to dwell with man, but the house must be first cleansed of man's selfish wrongs.

According to this descriptioon, which is plainly of the Zodiac (see illustration of the Zodiac), it has twelve gates or twelve angles, and each angle or sign represents one of the twelve tribes of Israel (i. e., the twelve different distinct natures).

Here is where we get the idea of birthstones, that is, to those born in certain signs, the gems attributed to that particular sign is more fortunate than to others.  Who has not heard of the unlucky opal, and yet for people born in Libra the opal is a fortunate stone, and for most people born in Aries.  Notice a person

## THE STORY OF THE ZODIAC.

is supposed to be most fortunate wearing the stone belonging to their own sign, and next to wear the stone belonging to the sign right opposite.

A few years ago a gentleman came to me and asked if I really thought it was unlucky to wear an opal. I told him yes, for some people, and lucky for others, according to what month born in. "Well," said he, "I gave my daughter an opal ring and she never saw a well day after, until my wife took the ring and gave my daughter another ring, and after that time my daughter got well and my wife was taken with the same disease and died of it."

I learned they were born in the same month of the year, but the opal belonged to a sign square to their sign. I followed this investigation in other cases and found similar results.

As the names of stones became changed and certain kinds of stones lost sight of, different astrologers, not putting much faith in the matter, assigned such and such birthstones to each month as they saw fit, or jewelers who knew nothing of astrology did this to help the sale of their goods.

I will now treat of the great city of New Jerusalem, or the new Zodiac.

In 1912 Uranus enters Aquarius, with his father, the sun; that is, the son of the sun God returned, for the first time in 26,000 years; and then begins the reign of this New Jerusalem. Let us hope this is only typical of the true return of a real individual Christ, or Son of God.

The cruel Pisces cycle of 2,000 years in which Christ the lamb of Aries said the night was coming on in which no man could work, and the Pisces cycle has been a selfish, money-loving cycle, but the better things are at hand.

The New Jerusalem, whose eastern side and first gate is Aries and gem, is jasper. Potter's Bible Encyclopedia says jasper is the diamond. This stands for overcomers. Aries people, though lamblike, are fierce warriors or conquerors, and reformers.

The second angle is Taurus, represented by the sapphire, a species of agate. This is a beautiful stone, represents sympathy and purity, but is so hard it is next to a diamond, but not having the cutting qualities of a diamond; if it cannot subdue it will destroy itself, because of its brittle nature. Taurus stands for the bull, the symbol of the sign. Though the bull is docile, when aroused he is so fierce that he is liable to smash everything before him or be smashed. Taurus people have not the shrewdness of Aries people. The emerald is also worn by Taurus people, without harm.

The third angle, or Gemini, whose symbol is the twins. The stone is chalcedony. This stone is a species of agate, and is found in almost all parts of the world and is one of the most useful of stones as it is wrought into all manner of useful and ornamental works of man. It is a good representative of the Gemini people, who can make themselves at home in all lands, and are so useful that they are seldom satisfied to stick at one kind of work, but want to carry a load on both shoulders and do a good many things all at once, and do them well.

This is the east side, or the quarter of love, called the intellectual quarter.

The three northern gates are, first the sign Cancer, the symbol, the crab; the fourth gate, represented by an emerald.

This stone, though a beautiful stone, is more directly an article of commerce than of real utility, though it can be made useful, and as a thing of commerce is of great value. The Cancer people are distinctly a commercial people, and always do best when residing near the sea coast, and while often excellent mechanics and manufacturers, they should always try to combine production with trade.

## THE STORY OF THE ZODIAC.

Leo, the fifth gate or angle, is symbolized by the Lion, and its stone is sardonyx.

This stone is of a very rich brown color; though hard, it is susceptible of the finest carvings and engravings. Like Leo people, its adaptability knows no limit. This is often represented as the onyx, which is the darker colored of the sardius family; and the cat's-eye is also worn by Leo people and is of the same nature.

The sixth angle is Virgo, the virgin, its stone the sardius, bearing the same description as the sardonyx, and the natures of the people are much alike except that Virgo people are more stubborn and yet less independent than Leo people. This ends the North side.

The west side consists of Libra, the first gate or seventh angle, its stone as crysolite or opal. This is really the most beautiful stone of the lot, and seems to have the most marked effect on those who cannot wear it, of all the stones, as opal sickness is always preceded by melancholy; and even Libra people, the handsomest people, as a whole, of the whole twelve signs, are also given to frequent spells of melancholy.

Scorpio, the second gate of the West side and the eighth sign, symbolized by the Scorpion, is represented by beryl.

This is a beautiful light blue stone, often found in large pieces, octagon in shape, and that is the eighth house, or sign, and stands for durability.

The third gate and ninth sign is Sagittarius, symbolized by the archer. The stone is the topaz. This is a beautiful yellow stone also of the beryl species, and stands for music. Sagittarius people are natural musicians, but seldom play by ear, always by note.

This closes the west side or quarter of wealth, or reproducing quarter.

The first gate of the south side is Capricornus, symbolized by the goat. This is the tenth sign, represented by the stone chrysoprasus, or gold stone. This is a beautiful white agate sprinkled with gold. How appropriate, a gold stone; and we judge of Capricornus, honor, business and dishonor. What will not people do for gold! Capricornus people are the greatest business schemers of the whole twelve signs.

The eleventh gate, or second gate of the south side, is Aquarius, the water-bearer, labor. The stone is the jacinth or ruby. This is the rarest and most expensive gem of all stones; though cheap imitations are plentiful, the real ruby is very scare and high priced. It represents purity. This sign stands for the highest and the lowest, and is the home of the son of the sun God, who is now to reign for a thousand years, and labor is to rule or rest for a thousand years.

The third gate of the south side, or twelfth sign, is Pisces, the fishes. The stone is the amethyst, a very rich and beautiful purple stone, though very common and plentiful, and there are more people born in this sign than any other.

This ends the south side or quarter of labor, or serving quarter.

There is a change of dispensation every two thousand years, and with each quarter the air sign represents the Lord's Sunday of one thousand years. "A thousand years is as a day and a day as a thousand years with the Lord." We are about to enter this New Jerusalem, this new dispensation, when honesty and justice will reign and the old song be realized: "Every day will be Sunday bye-and-bye." For we are about to pass through God's Sunday.

## WHAT THE NEW JERUSALEM WILL BE LIKE.

As this work has seemed to be for the purpose of massing every proof possible, scientific, materialistic and theistic, against the character, Christ, I now wish to take the other side and show the real Christ to be a character to emulate, and it does not matter whether there was one in the flesh or not. But this question is not new. The Bible writers themselves admit the discussion had been going on in their day, and that the fight of the creeds against the Christ religion was going on at the time of the writing of the books of the new testament, 150 years after the supposed birth of Christ.

I John, 4:1. "Beloved, believe not every spirit, but try the spirits whether they are of God: because many false prophets are gone out into the world.

I John, 4:2. "Hereby know ye the Spirit of God: Every spirit that confesseth that Jesus Christ is come in the flesh is of God."

If there had been no discussion of this thing, why this expression.

If Christ was resurrected, it was a case of reincarnation.

Let us now note the true nature of Christ and we shall find a lovable ideal character, created either in the flesh or in the ideal character, as an example for the uplifting of man; and it does not matter whether in the flesh or the ideal. The true lover of the character will not split hairs on that point, but will ask, Am I or you living as near as possible like that ideal character? And if we profess it and are not, we are falsifiers, liars.

Now let me prove Christ was opposed to the rich man and was and is the best friend the poor man ever had. If he was a Socialist in principle, those who are not Socialists, yet pretend to follow him, are falsifiers and dangerous enemies, or wolves in sheeps' clothing, or else the character and the history are contradictory.

## THE STORY OF THE ZODIAC.

In ancient times, the city where dwelt the king or ruler was virtually the nation.

The wealthy class of all ages has been the ruling class, and through their selfishness have destroyed the nation. They have, through the process of selfish rule divided the people into classes, and then encompassed, not only their own destruction, but the destruction of the nation.

It is silly to suppose the present age is the apex of civilization. We have had a much higher state of civilization than we now have, and, as Solomon said, "There is nothing new under the sun."

I have shown the Sphinx and the Pyramids are evidence that over 16,000 years ago there was a higher state of civilization than we now have.

The remains of the decayed civilization of China, of India, and of Egypt all testify to this fact, and that they all went down through the same cause—the folly and cruelty of the selfish wealthy classes.

The engine that produces this destruction is interest on money and class legislation, together with the dividing of the people into classes and denying the masses the right to rule themselves; and through the process of misrule, class rule becomes so corrupt the masses are compelled to rise, and the wealthy class, through its ill-gotten gains, causes the masses to destroy each other and finally through the process to exterminate their rulers and cause a retrograde in civilization.

In the ruins of all ancient civilization the evidence of class oppression is found, down to the class distinction in China and India today.

Think of it! Through no fault of your own to be ostracized and an outcast that no one of the supposed upper classes dare touch for fear of being contaminated.

No matter how intelligent or how cleanly, if you belong to the working class, among some of the tribes in India, you are a dreaded outcast, and this used to be carried to an extent of vile treatment that would not be extended to the lower animals.

Every once in awhile the people would arise and throw off the yoke; but, through the power of interest on money, the conditions would be quickly brought back. This was so well understood that interest on money was bitterly condemned for over 1,500 years after Christ, says "Murray on Usury," that no one dare openly advocate interest on money.

We are told in history that it was the wickedness of the people of Sodom and Gomorrah, of Tyre and Sidon, of Ninevah, of Babylon, of Carthage, of Jerusalem, and of Rome, that caused their downfall.

What constituted that wickedness?

Is it not plain that it is selfish brutishness and inhumanity of man, begot through a backward movement of civilization?

What is civilization?

Civilization cannot consist of a mere rise in mechanical development, but to the greatest good to the greatest number.

Great individual wealth of the few over the masses begets careless, selfish independence, and when the people object to this, political parties are organized and corruption in high places sets the example, and honesty becomes a byword. Then it is not a matter of did you commit the crime, but, did you get caught at it. All students of history will remember of the corrupt commercialism of Greece and ancient Sparta, and of the story of the boy who had stolen the fox, and while standing before the magistrate actually permitted the fox, which he had concealed under his tunic, to gnaw his vitals out, rather than to admit his guilt by exposing the fox. Whether true or not, it is illustrative of a horrible state of human depravity and selfishness.

All history shows corruption and dishonesty is grounded in the upper classes and that the church is their most pliant tool and ally and mode of deception; the press is the next greatest element of deception because of the power begot of wealth. The political and legal bodies are mere means to an end, as I shall prove by history.

The history of religious wars is a mere evidence of internal strife among themselves. The leaders fought for the spoils, and their deluded followers for sentiment that was created by falsehood and superstition.

The old Pagan Babylonian Society, organized by a harlot for the most fiendish and horrible purpose of the leading class, was a mere repetition of former similar societies. But, as every organization must contain some conscientious believers and workers that really lead the deluded masses, they naturally abhorred and exposed these corruptions. This always caused new religious bodies to arise, and then it became necessary to reorganize and get control of the masses.

This is usually done by pretending to accept the reformer's ideas, until they can get fully into control and then return to the corruption.

Look back at the Christian church. Christ was a labor leader, so poor he had no place to lay his head, Labor dare trust no other. Because of the people's poverty the Pagan church was the ruling power, and they sought to hold the masses down by the vilest persecutions imaginable—crucifixions, burning to the stake, burning the eyes out, throwing to wild beasts and every other form of intimidation. For all of this the Christian church grew so fast that the Pagan church went down until Constantine's time. He being a shrewd politician, advised the Pagans to accept the new religion until they could control the masses. This was done and our present Catholic church built out of the two churches. This church was so completely the tool of the monied ruling classes that it finally was at the head of state, as in the papal rule of the world.

## THE STORY OF THE ZODIAC.

Protestantism arose out of a discussion, as to certain forms and biblical translations.

We can see the same spirit of intolerance and church and political rule and methods manifest in church and politics today.

As these new bodies arose, they were naturally of the laboring class, and they spoke bitterly of the upper or wealthy classes and dared not trust them. Hence there were many labor leaders, like those spoken of in the forepart of this book; and, like Christ, who was so poor he had no place to lay his head, they dared not trust any other leader. I will give testimony of this in Biblical quotations. But first let me show how the courts have always been used to sustain the wealthy.

We are told in I Samuel, 8, that the judges sold themselves for filthy lucre, and then the people cried, "Give us a king, O Lord." God told them through Samuel he would give them a king, but the king would take their sons and their daughters, their lands and their vineyards and the best of all they had.

Now let us read Roland's History and he will tell you that Carthage fell through the corruption of the wealthy classes, and that after Scipio restored Hannibal to rule, Hannibal was compelled to impeach the whole bench of judges. Yet the wealthy classes forced Hannibal out of his country and he died an exile.

The Bible tells us that Pilot was a judge before whom Christ was brought, but he could find no guilt or fault with Christ and washed his hands of the whole affair. This should have been a great honor to Pilot had he refused to have anything more to do with it; but, instead, to please the high priest, Pilot gave up Christ, the labor leader, to die in place of a real criminal, who, it is said, was the son of a rich man. At any rate, it was Christ's offending that class of hypocrites in high places that caused

## THE STORY OF THE ZODIAC.

them to legally murder him, and in my great book, "What Is Coming," I have shown, from most remote times to the murder of Lincoln and Garfield, the people's defenders have been murdered by the monied classes.

Let me quote a little from the Bible in proof of the fact that worldly riches are the basis of all evil. Timothy, 6:10, says:

"THE LOVE OF MONEY IS THE ROOT OF ALL EVIL."

Here, then, is the acknowledgment—this is the basis of all crime. "Take thou no usury or increase."

There is no dodging this commandment, and the horror with which the lending of money for gain was looked upon is manifest in the twenty-second chapter of Ezekiel, which says for the taking of usury and greedily gaining one of another, God took from the Jews the land he had given their fathers for an everlasting inheritance.

The want of space forbids my quoting a hundredth part of the evidence against the taking of interest on money.

Christ was forever condemning the wealthy class. The only time he used force or sanctioned the use of force was when, with the scourge, he drove the money changers from the temple. Matthew 21:12.

That Christ was often making war on the churches and the money gatherers is manifest in Matthew 23:14: "But woe unto you scribes and pharisees, hypocrites; for ye devour widows' houses and for a pretence make long prayers; thereby ye shall receive the greater damnation.

"15. Woe unto you scribes and pharisees, hypocrites; for ye compass sea and land to make one proselyte, and when he is made ye make him twofold more the child of hell than yourselves."

"24. Ye blind guides, which strain at a gnat and swallow a camel."

## THE STORY OF THE ZODIAC.

How the churches of today are straining at the gnat of the slums and ignoring the great crime, the camel of interest on money, and the crimes of the trusts and monopolies that make slums.

Again: "But what went ye out for to see? A man clothed in fine raiment? Behold, they that wear soft clothing are in kings' houses." Matthew 11:8.

Mark 10:25: "It is easier for a camel to go through the eye of a needle, than for a rich man to enter into the kingdom of God."

In all history, the real studied criminal has come from the selfish well-to-do upper class; not the slums, which the church is forever hypocritically fighting. Though the assassination of rulers is generally laid to the lower or middle class, it is easily traceable to the upper class, as the trail of blood over the bloody stairway at the imperial palace of Russia testifies.

A beautiful comparison of this is found in President Lincoln's special message July 4th, 1861. In speaking of the welfare of the government, he says: "I am most happy to believe that the plain people understand and appreciate this. It is worthy of note that while in this government's hour of trial large numbers of those in the army and navy who have been favored with offices have resigned and proved false to the hand which had pampered them, not one common soldier or sailor is known to have deserted his flag."

This is a wonderful tribute to the plain people, the private soldiers. Out of about ten thousand troops receiving but $8.00 per month, readily obeyed the command of their officers while true to the flag, by those officers were offered great inducements to desert their flag, not a man deserted.

In his first annual message, December 3, 1861, and on other occasions President Lincoln warned the plain people of the endeavors that were being made and would be made to deprive them of their liberties and to destroy our government.

In my great book on finance, "What Is Coming," I
have shown many evidences of this, but let me go
back to Scripture.

In Ephesians 6:11-12 it shows where the trouble lay
in Christ's time. "Put on the whole armour of God,
that ye may be able to stand against the wiles of the
devil.

"For we wrestle not against flesh and blood, but
against principalities, against powers, against the
rulers of the DARKNESS OF THIS WORLD,
AGAINST SPIRITUAL WICKEDNESS IN HIGH
PLACES."

I have shown that the heart of man is about the
same the world over, except as greed for gain estab-
lishes false systems and warps the mind of man.
Thus the Jews were told that they might charge
interest, or usury, which is one and the same thing,
to those they wish to kill.

This spiritual wickedness in high places is rapidly
undermining the liberties of the American people,
corrupting society, raising a false standard of salaries
for notables at the expense of the taxpayer and the
underlying servant that must do the bulk of labor,
and has utterly destroyed the usefulness of the majority of church societies.

Seeing the rich man piling up millions he never
could honestly earn, or use, and which go to make
him so desirous of more, he too often deceives to
avoid his just share of taxes and resorts to most
shameful and dishonorable means to gain more
wealth, and his easy manner of acquiring wealth
stimulates such a desire for get-rich-quick schemes
that honesty is a byword and a laughing stock, and
the preacher will not attack this greatest of all
crimes, "Interest." Truly, "the love of money is the
root of all evil."

The two cuts show the evils of bonded indebted-
ness and the lack of humanity to man, but that is
often extended to the small horse but never to the
poor man; and the second cut, which shows the real

156

We give the long end of the evener to the small horse to make the big horse pull his share of the load. We are not so humain to our fellow man. Interest is the basis of all unreasonable profit or rent. It is the long end of the evener to the successfull man.

"The love of money is the root of all evil.'
"Take thou no usury or increase."
Leviticus XXV- 36

"Papa, what are all those men doing?"
"My son, they are trying to make two blades of grass grow where one grew before, and are so busy they have no time to scheme to steal the results of other men's toil."
"Papa, what is the big man doing?"
"He is scheming to get all of the blades of grass, and he has lots of time, for that is his business, and he is building a h——! for his posterity."
"What fools those mortals be."

producer's mind is so intent on his labors of production that he has no time to plot schemes of legal robbery and no time to stimulate a desire to do so, while the man of dollar marks has both time and is continually stimulating the desire for greed and greater gains.

The reason I have not quoted the story of Lazarus in Abraham's bosom and the rich man suffering in hades, is because it is not Christlike. It is probably an interpolation, to pander to the taste of the revengeful on one hand and to stimulate followers of the church on the other, with promises in a mythical heaven of what it was impossible to acquire in this life.

Here is the Christ principle: "Ye have heard that it hath been said, Thou shalt love thy neighbor, and hate thy enemy. But I say unto your, 'Love your enemies, bless them that curse you, do good to them that spitefully use you, and persecute you.'" Matthew 6:43-44.

What a contrast this is to the story of Lazarus and the rich man! What good could it do Lazarus, the rich man, God or man, to torture the rich man forever, while he was a mere child of circumstances and conditions?

It is true, God or intelligent nature may, and if the prophecies be true, will soon use harsh measures to remove the wealthy legal robbers and plotters of commercial slavery of their fellowman, and if the money-loaning class were not greed blind they would see their danger and begin to prepare for it, instead of stealing the people's rights of making money, and then lending back to the people on interest, until the annual increase of wealth is not enough to pay the interest on the $80,192,698,000 (eighty billion one hundred and ninety-two million six hundred and ninety-eight thousand) of indebtedness our last statistics say exists in this country, without counting private debts and open accounts.

## THE STORY OF THE ZODIAC.

When a financial panic comes, and it is too often brought on purposely, the values of property shrink, but the debts never; thus the system becomes legalized robbery.

The whole world is looking for Christ's second coming, and this time the Astrologer points to the parallel in the stars of the heavens, and the time is about up.

Before, Christ came riding on an ass. He was poor, had no place to lay his head. His disciples were communists, or socialists, and had everything in common. He was despised by the rich, murdered by law, at the command of the high priests.

Christ, let us hope and believe he comes in the flesh, but know he comes in principle, and his friends, by the million, without knowing it perhaps, are preparing the way for him. "And the stars of the heavens (kings, princes and money lords, that is their power) shall fall to the earth like a tree casting its untimely fruit, shaken by a mighty wind." See Revelation.

So much to pave the way to the description of the New Jerusalem. The thousand-year reign of Justice, when no man shall have an advantage, one over another.

This does not mean that because it requires an engineer and a mule to build a railroad that the mule shall be taken into the parlor or to the table of the engineer, or that he shall have a stall so gorgeous beyond his capacity to understand, and at the necessary expense of justice to the engineer; but it does mean that the engineer shall not, through privileges, steal the oats from the mule, or the food and raiment from his own fellows, who are his equals or more and entitled to as much as he is.

This time Christ will come strong enough to establish his socialistic system of justice to all. It will not be in the misty somewhere, but here; and with no dirty red flag, but in this country, which God said through his astrological prophets he would give to

## THE STORY OF THE ZODIAC.

his people, and under our heaven-born banner
snatched from the skies, and first symbolized by the
twelve sons of Ishmael. Genesis 25. Again by the
twelve sons of Jacob, who represented the twelve
tribes of Israel, and again by the twelve disciples,
and in the heavens by the twelve signs of the Zodiac,
and again by the twelve religious societies forming
twelve colonies that fled to this country for liberty
of thought, from 1600 to 1682. It was twelve colonies, not thirteen, as Georgia did not come in until
after the war began, and there were but twelve signers of the Declaration of Independence, and the first
banner flung to the breee by the immortal Paul Jones
bore but twelve stars. See explanation in "What Is
Coming."

## A SONNET TO THE FLAG.
### OUR HEAVEN BORN BANNER

When Freedom sought an emblem true,
  A banner from the God of Right,
She tore from out the azure blue
  A raiment from the robes of night,
As if her cap from heaven's store
  Was set with glorious stars of white.

"Eternal Vigilance" 'tis said
  "The price of Liberty" was given.
The stripes the vigilant must wear
  Were also symbolized in heaven.

The red was found in crimson glow
  Between the sun set and the night,
While purity of white we know
  Is found at dawn of early light.

There will be no necessity of anyone working more
than four hours per day, as a just distribution will
take the place of the wasteful selfish system we now
have. Everybody will be studying out schemes for
public good, knowing honorable reward awaits them.

It has been said the socialist scheme is visionary
and could not exist. But the new planetary conditions are rapidly paving the way for the great
change.

## THE STORY OF THE ZODIAC.

Undoubtedly new forms of cities will be established, in shape like the picture of the Zodiac, with a grand center large enough for all public works, with twelve roads leading out like spokes to a wheel, and as the city expands block after block will be added; the streets and alleys separating the blocks will run in circles around the city. The people will rule and their votes will decide everything, and their representatives will be merely executive officers.

As injustice, in high places more than anywhere else, is the greatest cause of crime, there will be no necessity for prisons, though asylums will exist for unfortunates of all kinds, including selfish insanity.

In this country it will not be necessary for wars, as most of the rich men will see it will be a greater blessing for themselves and families to fall into the new order of things and become benefactors of the human race than to support a false system and continually wrong their fellowman. Of course someone will kick against the pricks and must suffer the consequences, the same as Ananias of old. See Acts 5:1-2.

There will be no necessity of a great change of government, for governments are always necessary, and ours is the best that ever existed and our flag the most beautiful and representative flag. All that is necessary is to educate the people, and unless this privilege of education is interfered with no trouble need ever be experienced in correcting the existing evils, and it is folly to expect to correct them all at once; but the greatest evil of them all, interest on money, should be corrected first, and if for a time it be necessary that money be borrowed and loaned, then let the government make and loan all the money at the lowest possible percent, and whatever interest there is accumulated will come back to the whole people, and not give such a great advantage to a few nor perpetuate false values based upon interest.

DO YOU FAVOR CHRIST'S SYSTEM OR ARE YOU A PRETENDER?

## THE STORY OF THE ZODIAC.

Since this book has been put in type the question has been asked me, "Do you not think that if the law of evolution and progress is right, that astrology was necessary to the ancients and that faith is a step forward and to go back to astrology is wring, since going backward is a part of the forbidden fruit?"

My answer to this is: Astrology is a science, and there never has been an honest command to drop astrology. In fact I have shown it was first the corrupt priesthood who made war on astrology.

I do not oppose faith; in fact faith has always been necessary. Christian Science, Mental Science, Hypnotism, and other branches of Occult Science, prove, by their examples, that religion has not got a monopoly in faith. Everything goes to show that all the efforts of man would be fruitless without faith. Man could not keep the food on his stomach without faith. The farmer would not plant his field if he had no faith. Our Spiritualist friends find they can get no good results without faith. Nothing of the affairs of man would be successful without faith.

I ask which seems the nearest right, to accept with blind faith what seems to be merely an allegory, or to manfully seek the truth through a mathematical science that seems to have been cast off by a lot of dishonest priests?

Again I am asked, "Do you not think one is apt to get on best who seeks to harmonize with his fellow man rather than to antagonize all?"

I answer, most assuredly I do; hence this closing chapter to show I do not strike at individuals or individual business but at false systems; so let us be friends. You have a right to your opinion, I have a right to mine.

## CLOSING CHAPTER.

In this I ask that no reader think that I desire
to attack any individual or the business of any individual, banker, saloonkeeper, judge, lawyer, preacher, or the organizer of trusts.

Human nature is much alike the world over—we
all love money and power, and when tempted and
surrounded by circumstances we are so circum-
scribed we are hardly able to do different from what
we do do. I myself lay no claims of being better
or wiser than other men.

A large horse may pull a load that a small horse
cannot, and he requires more food, but no better
stable or grooming.

A railroad magnate may know how to assemble
the capital required to build the road, also how to
expend the capital to the best advantage, or even
in this he must trust largely to others. But with
all, what would he do without the mechanics who
build the engines, the cars, or make the rails. He
could not do either one, nor could he grade the
road or lay the rails. Then why should he become
a millionaire and use his road to raise the price
of commodities to that labor who created the rails
and rolling stock, which he could no more create
than they could manage the road. Every man is his
brother's keeper. It requires one man to take care
of another, the world over, and we are all selfish
and each would like to take the place of the successful man. But should we do it or allow him to take
advantage of the masses? No! No!! No!!! It is
false system, not men, I wish to attack. Far be it
from me to desire to assail any man, newspaper,
church, priest, or charity, or advise anyone to with-
hold support from anything that is doing good.

The press will not publish a labored article of
value on Astrology that I may write and present
them, but they will publish some sensational stuff

## THE STORY OF THE ZODIAC.

that would only tend to injure the great science of Astrology, and this is largely because the church for ages has put a ban on the practice of Astrology.

And today by Astrology I can prove the running of the mighty machinery of the universe, the work of the Master Mind, and I can make the dark spots in Scripture, which they stumble over or hush up, so plain a child can understand them. But they look upon my science with contempt and scorn and would not let me in their churches, though I could show them the story of the Christian religion is enacted by the Sun and Stars every year. Hence I must strike back and say, "Either admit the truth of the great science of Astrology or admit the whole story of the Old and New Testaments is an allegory based upon Astrology."

The careful reader of this book must take one horn of the dilemma or the other, if he be a reasoner. But individually let us be friends. If you do not feel so or feel individually offended, I beg your pardon for offending you, but not for presenting the truth.

I cannot expect all to agree with me—one has as much right to his opinion as another; but as human progress is made over decaying ideas and systems, and "old things shall pass away and all things become new," none of us should hesitate to read and reason.

The twelve pages of brief character readings should convince any person of the truth of the science. If you want more evidence send 50 cents for my "Universe," or 50 cents for my book "What Is Coming," or 25 cents for "The Great Prophecy," or what is better, send $1.00 with date of birth and get your horoscope, with good and evil periods of life. This should be proof of the truth of Astrology.

Since "BIBLE ASTROLOGY" was written I have been asked: "If what you have written destroys a man's faith, WHAT HAVE YOU GOT TO GIVE HIM IN ITS PLACE°"

My natural answer must be the truth.

Some people say, the truth should not always be told, thus claiming a well-told lie is better than the truth. In that case I must ask the question, Faith in what°

The Mohammedan would say, "In Mohammed."

The Buddhist would say, "In Buddha."

The Christian would say, "In Christ and church teachings."

The ancient Sun worshippers would say, "In the Sun."

Some of the ancient Egyptians, "Chine's."

Japanese and Scandinavians would say, "In Apies, the White Bull."

Certain idol worshipers would say, "In Oden or Wooden."

So you can go on to the various orders of belief, all of which are thories, the outgrowth of Astrological Allegory.

All declare, and many believe, theirs the right and only theory, and if you say anything against their pet theory you are a candidate for punishment of some sort. They never stop to think one is as likely to be right as another, or has as much right to his belief as another.

If no one had ever dared to declare his right to differ from another there would have never been but one form of belief or religion, that of worship of sticks and stones or idols.

Any man who investigates must see that the chief purpose of all such organizations was originally to

benefit some would-be leader, and their final uses
are to make the small fry supporters of ambitious
leaders, and lastly of self constituted "Divine right"
Kings or other politicians.

Of course the waves of religion rise and fall with
the waves of civilization.

It should be manifest that the highest forms of
religion should teach the divine in natural law, for
the betterment of mankind.

The very weakness of all forms of modern religion,
even to Christianity, stamp them as man-made forms
or theories, based upon older, if not better theories.

The very idea of the God of the universe, who is
supposed to make nothing in vain, makes untold
millions of human beings, whom many of the lower
animals could put to shame, and then saves a very
few of them and sends the rest to eternal damnation,
so the greatest part of his work is worse than in
vain. Not only this, but he sends all that is good
and beautiful to die in pain for these poor creatures
that, with the wave of his hand, as it were, he could
make perfect, and save from such dreadful torture.

They say this God is merciful, yet there is no man
so cruel that he would let an enemy suffer, so ter-
ribly, for long.

Would this God be so careful to write a book as a
guide to man and then be so careless as to let so
many of its parts be lost? Or that it would require
to be retranslated so many times, or require such a
vast number of interpretations with conflicting
views, creating contending factions, ready to send
everyone to perdition who differs from them in
views?

Let us review a little of THE HISTORY OF
ASTROLOGY, RELIGION AND FREEMASONRY.

The most prominent of ancient religion was based
upon Astrology.

## THE STORY OF THE ZODIAC.

This would seem to be the most reasonable religion, because it was based upon nature. Besides, all RELIGION, MYTHOLOGY, FREEMASONRY and consequently all secret organizations, were based upon Astrology and were apparently originated for the betterment of man. But the real purpose of their organization was to gain followers and supporters of ambitious leaders.

Astrology and Sun worship had to be taught by men of intellect, reasoners and philosophers; hence they were called "wise men."

This was nature's religion. These men taught the "Golden Rule" thousands of years before the Christians, Mohammedans, Buddhists or the followers of Zoreaster thought of it.

These wise men taught that it was the Golden Rule that *"One man's rights must cease where another man's rights begin."*

This, if followed closely, would bring a heaven on earth.

If all of the machinery of religion, secret socities, governments and war were turned to teach and enforce this principle, we would soon have heaven right here.

Instead of cumbering the law books with useless laws to prohibit, the attention of man should be drawn to sustain man in his rights, always starting with "The greatest good to the greatest number."

The next idea should be to protect the weak against the strong.

THE BASIS OF THE RIGHTS OF MAN IS:

First, the individual has a right to as much of nature's gifts as he can make use of for his needs, and no more. If these gifts are limited, the only place for human judgment would come in as to the decisions of their respective needs.

He that takes more than his immediate wants demand is either a robber or a deceiver, or is forced to

### THE STORY OF THE ZODIAC.

do so by a robber system he readily sees will force him to starve if he does not. In the latter case it is the system that requires correcting.

No man would uphold a person in forcibly taking from another what that other had produced without giving an equivalent in return, as that would be called ROBBERY.

No man will claim there is more than two ways of producing wealth to supply the wants of man, and these are through natural gifts or labor.

Goods left behind by a dying man should revert back to nature's store, otherwise they artificially increase the powers of one whose rights must cease where the other man's rights begin.

The moment a man has a right to accept the goods of the dead he is laying the foundation of a privileged class, who are more dangerous than a pack of wolves, because it is an understood right to exterminate the wolves, while the weak are called upon to sustain a privileged class, which in the end undermine individual rights, destroy liberty and make justice a farce.

A man is excusable for taking advantage of a false system, for no man can reform a false system alone. But he is doubly guilty of crime who preaches and upholds a false system and then takes advantage of it.

It is every man's duty to try to reform a bad system.

He that tries to chain the mind on an imaginary heaven is blinding the eyes to a possible heaven on earth. In the presence of such keep your hand on your pocket.

He that is always trying to make laws to prohibit others is really in need of a restraining influence himself.

Unnatural inequality is the result of selfishness. If such things exist in heaven, it is no better than earth.

## THE STORY OF THE ZODIAC.

Christ had no place to lay his head.

Either stop preaching Christ or sell what you have and given to the poor, then follow Him.

Better still, remove the laws that make a privileged class, and you will soon have everybody trying to make a heaven on earth.

He that is fit to live in a heaven on earth will be fit to live in any other heaven.

He that is forever harping about a future hell for other people will be the one mostly likely to tumble into it, if not the most deserving of it.

He that is trying to better the conditions of man on earth will be hailed as a good citizen in heaven, if there be such a place.

He that builds stone temples to the gods while the people are without homes is a fit subject for a sycophant to a robber king, who has declared he has a divine right to rob and rule.

He that is able to build worlds will hardly ask a man to build him a temple of stone, before he has a house to cover his own head.

If man would build perfect temples to God, let him help to make perfect men on earth.

A system that permits man to gather to himself more of the products of nature, or to take from labor its results without giving an equivalent in return, is a robber system.

From the first attempt of the physical bully, or the political trickster, to establish himself as a ruler, or to establish systems of interest or profit, started a privileged class, and the church became an instrument to deceive labor for the benefit of greed.

THE PRIESTS AND TEACHERS OF ANCIENT TIMES naturally became a powerful class. The governing class was quick to take advantage of it.

What temptation could not do, extermination was called on to do.

Under rotten political conditions the old religions became rotten. Honest men now began teaching the people Astrology. This enraged the priesthood, and religious strife was the result. Of course the political powers upheld the priesthood, and this made it very hard for the people.

New forms of religion have always had to struggle against the prejudice of old forms, but nature seemed to provide against this by making "Persecution the seed of the church."

Free Masonry became a new form of religion. They were pressed so hard by the old forms and the governing classes that they were compelled to seek meeting places in the mountains and out of the way places. This was the first of Free Masonry.

At this time both the church and Free Masonry conducted their services along the lines of Astrology. I have shown this clearly in "Bible Astrology." The explanation of hades, where the worm dieth not, which is the sign Sagitarius. The houses and mansions in the skies, which are the divisions of the heavens and earth, and many other things.

Now let me refer to the astrology of the Free Masons.

On account of the Masons being a labor organization they mingled the emblems of their trade with those of astrology. Hence the very first thing was to take the arch of the circle, which is astronomical, and form an arch of it. In this they placed the keystone, emblazoned with the symbols of their trades, and astrology. The workman's tools are the compass and square.

In the center the capital letter G. What does the G stand for?

When Pat was asked what it stands for, he said: "Why the devil can't you see that the compass and square are the carpenter's tools, and av course the G stands for gimlets."

## THE STORY OF THE ZODIAC.

The Mason says it stands for God and Geometry.

Astrology is purely a mathematical science, and geometry is one of the basic principles of mathematics.

What means the term the fourth dimensions, which is length without depth or breadth? Such a line must eventually become a circle, aye, encompasses the whole.

Not only Free Masons but ancient religious forms made frequent reference to the 47th problem of Euclid.

No man has ever been able to add to or detract from one preposition of Euclid.

Now let us follow out a few of their expressions they willingly or unintentionally give to the public.

As I am not a Mason, I must rely on my observation. I have no desire to do them harm by exposure. which of course I could not do; for, dear reader, if you are a member of any secret organization you already know that the main secret is that there is no secret except the grips and passwords, which is not to wrong the public but to protect their meetings from the disturbance of outside influences.

Surely the Masons have got nothing they need be ashamed of. At the present their teachings are the same as those of the church, and nothing is more beautiful than the ideal character of Christ. The only thing that I object to in either is that they pretend to follow a meek and lowly master but instead serve the devil of a money god.

See farther on why the Church and Free Masons quarreled.

The compass must be used to draw the circle, yet it is a mechanical tool.

The square. though a mechanical tool, is also one of the chief figures in astrology.

The trowel, the chisel and the mallet are tools frequently spoken of, which show that Masonry was originally a labor organization; but the strongest

## THE STORY OF THE ZODIAC.

evidence and the most interesting reference is that which recognizes the right of labor to what it produces, and to that of no other man's production, even though he found it.

In the Mark Masons' degree these words are found:

A candidate for initiation receives a key stone, which has not the mark of the craft upon it. The examining officer after applying the square says it is neither oblong nor square; he asks, "Is this your work?" The answer is, "No, sir." The next question, "Where did you get it?" Answer, "I picked it up in the quarry." The officer replies, "You picked it up in the quarry. This explains the matter. You have been loitering, and now impose another man's labor on the overseer. This deserves the severest punishment."

Here is a grand expression of justice, that one man has no right to appropriate the labor of another, without giving an equivalent in return, even though he find it. But how many of our Free Mason brothers think of this?

Probably about as many as there are of the church people who practice the beautiful teachings of Christ. Both teachings are grand and beautiful, but when taught and not practiced they become a deception and a snare.

In their opening prayer, we find the following:

"Most holy and glorious God, the architect of the universe." So here you find more evidence of a labor organization, based upon the foundation of structure.

Let us here compare the shape of the temple with the zodiac.

In the 21st chapter of Revelations we get a description of the New Jerusalem, descending out of heaven.

It is four square with 12 gates—3 on the east, 3 on the north, 3 on the west and 3 on the south.

Solomon's temple was built after this description, and the Free Mason's temple is built after this description, and the writer of Revelations undoubtedly referred to the new formation of the Zodiac and the new condition of things after the Sun has passed over into Aquarius or the recision of the Equinox.

Since Solomon's time the Free Masons have closed the north side of the temple. They give as their reason for doing so that in their search for more light they travel to the east; so they speak of light in the west and in the south at noon and in the east, but there is no light in the north. But this is not the real reason for Solomon closing the north side of the temple. Three tribes of the Jews never crossed the river Jordan, and this was the reason for the closing of the three north gates.

All this talk of the New Jerucalem and the temple is merely a description of the 12 signs of the Zodiac.

All of their talk of travel from west to east is a symbol of the motion of the planets from west to east.

In Bible Astrology I have shown the story of the murder of the Sun and his rebirth on the 25th day of December is the same story of Christ's death and resurrection.

The Free Masons have a similar story in the betrayal and death of Hyram Abiff, except that where in the case of Christ the people smote themselves on the breast in despair. But in the case of Hyram Abiff, King Solomon cries in despair, "Is there no help for the widow's son?" or similar words.

Then Hiram Abiff was not resurrected. Otherwise the stories are similar, showing they were taken from planetary movements.

Note here God is called the great architect. Christ was a carpenter, often called the master or master builder. Hiram Abiff was the chief builder or master workman.

So we see the frequent reference to the master, by both church and Masonry, stamp them as of astrological origin.

Let me call attention again to the basing of both organizations upon the temple and, farther back, upon the Zodiac.

On the east you have Aries, Taurus and Gemini; on the north, Cancer, Leo and Virgo; on the west, Libra, Scorpio and Sagittarius; on the south, Capricornus, Aquarius and Pisces . Now note the trinity of the Zodiac. There are three signs on a side; there are three fire signs, three air signs, three earth signs, and three water signs.

We require a compass to draw the circle. Then the term of squaring the circle originated with astrology. Draw a line from the first degree of Aries to the first degree of Cancer, then to the first degree of Libra, thence to the first degree of Capricornus, thence to the first degree of Aries, and you have a perfect square of 90 degrees on each side. Follow this through each sign of the Zodiac and you have squared the circle in an astrological sense of meaning.

I can also give a mathematical form of squaring the circle, but it is out of place here.

Now note the Free Masons' temple, square, 12 doors. They use the compass and square, and the first step in Masonry is to accept the three great lights—the Bible, the square and the compass.

Again their reference to the east, west and south.

They have three moveable jewels—their reference to earth, chalk and charcoal.

All of this springs from the trinity in the Zodiac or temple made without hands.

The ancients considered man made in the image of his Creator, the Zodiac, the visible representative of God. Space is filled with atoms. Man is com-

## THE STORY OF THE ZODIAC.

posed of thinking entities. The king, soul or master builder is in the Solar Plexus, or abdominal brain. This is the real God principle in man.

The balancing faculty in man, or the second part of the trinity, is in the cerebelum at the base of the brain. Wound or attack this, and man's reason is dethroned.

The third part of the trinity, or the perceptives, is in the pineal gland at the top of the head just over the eyes.

This is the sixth sense, now so rapidly developing, preparing man for the new world to develop as the Sun advances into Aquarius.

The real trinity of God is the universal principle, the father. The Sun, ruler of our solar system, Uranius, the great spiritual planet, or only begotten son of the Sun, i. e., moves in a different manner than the other planets. He is about to commence his reign of a thousand years.

The Jews were Sun worshipers, their old prayer books still contain the figure of the Zodiac. The Sun was their Lion of Judah, the 12 signs of the Zodiac were his 12 deciples. Pisces, with its symbol of two fishes makes a fine basis for the allegory of Peter and John, Christ's Fishermen Deciples.

Now you have in the Bible the frequent use of the trinity, such as faith, hope and charity. "Ask and ye shall receive, seek and ye shall find, knock and it shall be opened unto you."

This is typified by every secret organization, who give three knocks as a signal before giving the password. Thus you see, if you have all of the so-called secrets of Free Masonry, or any other order, you cannot get into their lodges without the password. and no honest man would want to. Neither would he want to give their secrets away if he could. It is not my purpose to wrong my friends the Free

## THE STORY OF THE ZODIAC.

Masons, or the Church either, for the matter of that. It is merely a search for truth that I use what they have themselves given to the public.

With my limited knowledge of Free Masonry I could go on and show vast numbers of points of evidence to prove that the order is based on the Bible, and they do not deny it, and the Church and the Bible are both founded on astrology. So far, so good, for what is more beautiful than the ideal character of Christ and the moral teachings of the Christian religion, or the Masonic rites, as taught to their candidates. But alas, "How art the mighty fallen!"

I have shown why ancient Masonry split off from the Church, as it became necessary for labor to protect itself against the corrupt priesthood.

Let me say right here that with all of the faults laid at the door of the Catholic Church, it looks out for the laboring class of its own people better than all of the other churches put together. But this is like the Masons. It is exclusive, and the world should be a brotherhood.

Think of the Good Samaritan stooping down to the suffering Publican and inquiring, "Are you a Free Mason, or an Odd Fellow?" Or, "Are you a Catholic or a Protestant?"

When politicians found they could not scare or bribe Free Masons, for the purpose of breaking up or controlling their organization, they sent spies in to become members. This caused a beautiful symbol to be shown every candidate, and that is the strongest kind of form of structure, which is a circle with a triangle inside. By secrecy their order could not be broken; it must be through treason from within.

This method of destroying ancient Free Masonry had its counterpart in the methods of the old Pagan Church adopting the confessional, which in a modified form our Catholic friends use today. But it was originated for the purpose of betraying labor to the wealthy masters.

It should show to every reader of this work the necessity to guard any just principle with manhood and integrity, and to make character the standard of honor, and not dollars and cents, as is now done.

Both Free Masonry and the Church went into decay, because of their own rottenness. Something had to be done, so instead of the story of the Zodiac, the God, the Sun and the Uranian effects. The Church turned it to the worship of God. An allegorical Son and an imaginary Holy Ghost.

The writers of the New Testament thoroughly understood the rejected stone would yet become the chief stone of the corner or structure.

The Pagan Church apparently went down, but came up in the new form of the Christian Church, preserving nearly all of their forms and ceremonies, including a relic of the confessional, which had been rejected by the laboring class, as the Church was not altogether trusted. Hence Free Masonry again came to the front, but this time organized exclusively along the Jewish line of the building of the temple. But alas! we find its organizers were the tricksters of kings, serving a "Most Worshipful Master."

As the Church was organized for the same purpose, as is proven by the fact that it became such a political machine that the Pope himself became a temporal monarch, the Church nearly always favored wealth, and does so to this day. Even the typical church of the world, St. Peter's of Rome, was originally built in honor of Jupiter, the Astrological God of Wealth.

If all this be true, why the strife between Free Masonry and Catholicity?

To answer this we must go back to the Babylonian period, and then be brief.

I must admit my article is somewhat fragmentary or scattered, as our sources of information are not

## THE STORY OF THE ZODIAC.

in a connected history and must be gathered in fragments and connected, or put in proper shape.

The rise and fall of religious forms of ancient times were so frequent and so bitter it is hard to put them just where they belong, except in a general way.

During the existence of old Babylon the privileged classes became so overbearing, so rotten, that the laboring classes rebelled and reformed Masonry under the ancient order.

All religious organizations had sunk into mere forms and ceremonies.

It was this rottenness and corruption that destroyed all love of country or patriotism which enabled Syrous of Persia to easily take Babylon.

A secret society, composed of the ignorant classes, led on by the privileged class, established themselves under the name of "The Mystery of Babylon." Its creation and purpose was for the rule of the world.

This society took on a religious phase, and practiced the old astrological religion, to deceive and control the small-fry, so that the leaders could enjoy all of the luxuries and debauchery that was denied to the small fry. They enjoyed it under religious rites as priests and church leaders. It was this terrible rottenness that caused the labor organization to be reformed and a strife between them and the Mystics was the result. The Mystics, or Pagan Church, as it was afterward called, were originally sun worshipers, and their saints all had the halo around the head, the same as you now see around the head of the picture of Christ. All of the forms and ceremonies of the present Catholic church were practiced by the old Pagan church.

This Pagan church had a college of pontiffs, numbering seventy members, with its Supreme Pontiff or Pope. The Catholic church has the same.

As elsewhere stated, the Pagans adopted a new system of Astrology, which required a key that was

## THE STORY OF THE ZODIAC.

intrusted to one Peter Roma and no one could practice this system until he got the key of Peter.

'This afterward gave rise to the story of the Pope receiving his authority from Peter and that Peter holds the key to heaven.

The Pagan Pope wore the miter and was called infallible. In fact, my authority goes on to show every form of the Catholic church was taken from the old Pagan church. He also gives the years each form was adopted by the Catholic church.

The Pagan church went to such high excesses in Pagan Rome that it became such a stench in the nostrils of the senators that they felt compelled to expel them from the bounds of the Roman republic.

The Catholic priesthood even followed this example of debauchery, and sold indulgence.

It was at the time of the corruption of the Pagan priesthood in Rome that the honest priesthood sought to save the world by writing the books of the New Testament, giving us the allegorical character Christ, and giving it as taking place 200 years before these books were written. This took at once, and became so popular that the Pagan church, for a time, threw up its organization and pretended to become Christian, actually teaching the beautiful Christian doctrine, and of course won the people to it—and the masses of the Catholic people are honest in their convictions, as is also the masses of the priesthood, and the same may be said of Free Masons. But let us here see whether away up somewhere these institutions, as well as leaders of the Protestant churches, are not conspiring against the liberties of the masses of the people. Is it not proven by the great conspiracy of crowned heads?

In 1828 Prof. Samuel F. B. Morse, the inventor of the American telegraph, resided in Italy. He there learned of a conspiracy among the crowned heads of Europe, with the Pope at the head, to destroy the American republic. This work had been going

## THE STORY OF THE ZODIAC.

on for a long time, but a meeting was held January 30, 1829, at Vienna, Austria. The Emperor of Austria presided and in his remarks he said:

"As long as I live I will oppose a will of iron to the progress of liberal opinions.

"The present generation is lost, but we must labor with zeal and earnestness to improve the spirit of that to come. It may require a hundred years. I am not unreasonable, I give you a whole age; but you must work without relaxation."

Although this was a secret meeting, within a year it was learned that $100,000 had been sent to the United States to further this object. That was a very large sum of money for those times.

Anyone who has read the Hazzard Circular and other evidence of a great conspiracy in my book "What Is Coming" cannot doubt the conspiracy is still at work.

Let us remember that Free Masonry had gone down very low and the church had been very bitter against it, and that about this same time Masonry began making great strides. It was then exposed by one William Morgan, who was supposed to have been killed by the Masons. Since that time the church has not been so bitter against Masonry, and what the public knows of Masonry it seems to be organized along the same lines as the church.

Now the thinker must naturally ask himself: Is there an understanding between the great moguls of Masonry and church to act together to hold the masses down as long as possible for the benefit of trusts and money lords?

Of course no sane man would for one moment suppose the masses of our good and pure-minded Masons or church people would submit to being used or influenced for such purposes. But I must ask them to stop and think and study, before accepting the teachings and dogmas of any religious doctrine

## THE STORY OF THE ZODIAC.

or society, and ask whether they can do right to a brother while holding another mortal as superior and deserving of unearned position and wealth.

The Babylonians were well up in astronomy and astrology. It was they more than any other nation that corrupted the church and ancient astrology. It was the Babylonians who established our system of divisions in the time of day, into hours, minutes and seconds, after the divisions of the Zodiac into signs, degrees, minutes and seconds.

Labor was well organized and even agitated the 8-hour system—8 hours for recreation or devotion, 8 hours for sleep, and 8 hours for work. This was symbolized by a 24-inch guage, which was originally divided into inches to represent the 24 hours of the day.

Masonry sought to conceal its work, which angered the priesthood, who demanded that everything come under the confessional.

As both were working under astrological rules, and by the Helio Centric system, as they understood the rotundity of the earth at that time, that is, that the Sun was the central figure of our system.

The priesthood sought to prove Masonry wrong, and so adopted a system making the Earth the center round which the Sun, Moon and planets revolved. This is called the Geo-Centric system.

The Helio-Centric system makes the first degree of Libra the head of the Zodiac, while the Geo-Centric system made the first degree of Aries the head of the Zodiac.

The Helio system calculated aspects from the Earth, the Geo system from the Sun.

There were other changes the priesthood wrought, which enabled them while talking of one thing to mean something else. This kind of astrology required a key, which was intrusted to one Peter Ravell, and this afterward became the foundation of

## THE STORY OF THE ZODIAC.

the allegory of St. Peter being intrusted with the keys of heaven. No one could study astrology who did not get the key of Peter.

The Masons practiced the old system and in a measure exposed the new. This caused a clash, and started the people to thinking both systems were false, and really did more to destroy confidence in astrology than anything else. Finally something had to be done to deceive the people and gain their confidence; hence the priesthood wrote the books of the New Testament and created the allegory of the Son of God, instead of the Sun God.

The Masons had long been teaching the story of Hiram Abiff. The Church hoped to win back the laboring class by this new religion, of a meek and lowly master, who like the working men had no place to lay his head. This was a more enticing character than Hiram Abiff.

Let it be remembered that the Sun is apparently murdered through the treachery of Venus, and these allegorical characters are both murdered through treachery.

This idea of Hiram Abiff of Solomon's time, or of Christ the Messiah, born of a virgin, had its parallel in Babylon or even in Egypt, so far back that history fails to find a date for its origin.

The 25th of March is celebrated in the Church of Rome for the "Annunciation of the Virgin," or the miraculous conception of Christ. The same day was observed in Pagan Rome in honor of Cybele, the mother of the Babylonian Messiah, who was also slain by treachery, like the Son, like Christ, like Hiram Abiff.

The Old Testament gives us Jacob blessing his 12 sons, but really giving us the attributes of the 12 signs of the Zodiac.

There probably never were 12 tribes who were descendents of 12 sons, but there was no doubt 12 divisions or armies of the Jews, organized along astrological lines. It was when they took Palestine and began reorganizing and building their chief structure that the three doors of the north side were closed because of the three army corps, called tribes, who remained on the north side of the river Jordan. Remember this was hundreds of years before the Christian era, when it became necessary to reorganize Masonry as well as the Church.

After the Romans took Jerusalem Roman astrology took on new life, and when the Church and Masonry became so rotten, it was the honest factions of the priesthood who sought, through allegory, to restore confidence; hence the Savior was pictured as a beautiful character, who taught the people not to look out for tomorrow.

Remember, had they been taught economy the rich could not have got the products of labor; had they the system we have to-day they would have been taught to put their money in the bank at three per cent without security, and borrow it back at seven per cent with gilt-edged security. But this same character is afterward made to complain that he had no place to lay his head. This, of course, was to make poverty-sticken labor contented—the same as the promise of idleness and mansious in the skies, if they meekly submitted to robbery here.

With the revival of the new Christian Church, the priesthood resorted to the old trick of deceiving the people with foreign tongues, and astrology was generally condemned. The war then went on between Church and Masonry, until the Church began quarreling among themselves about what books of the Bible should be used. This continued until, between Catholicity and Protestantism, the world was deluged in blood.

It is an old saying that "When rogues fall out there is a chance for honest men." Under these conditions liberty of thought has got such a start that it will not be crushed down again for a thousand

## THE STORY OF THE ZODIAC.

years, or while the planet Uranus reigns. Yet all of this past strife was right when rightly understood.

Wherever Christianity has gone it has left its trail of blood.

Ancient Peru had 37,000,000 happy people, not a criminal or a pauper in the land, an almshouse or a prison, but they were making no progress. Pizarro went in there under the pretense of Christianizing and civilizing them. The old, happy Peruvians are now dead and in their place are 7,000,000 of wretched people, with modern Christianity and civilization, with all of its cussedness.

When America was discovered the Indians are said to have been independent and happy, but they were savages. Today the good Indians are all dead, and there are a few called civilized and Christianized with all of the vices of man.

The grand Christian nation, Russia, just marched its armies through the churches, while on their way to despoil an innocent heathen nation. They were whipped and taught humanity by another little heathen nation who has settled down to peaceful pursuits while the people of the big Christian nation. are murdering each other.

It is said Japan is rapidly becoming Christianized. If that be true and of such Christianity, God help Japan.

When the priesthood began to turn astrology into allegory they made some terrible blunders. They cut out what they thought they safely could of astrology and reincarnation and substituted the imaginary heaven, with its eternal idleness and mansions, and to frighten the timid they drew a picture of an eternal hell of torment, not thinking how ridiculous it was to teach man to love his enemies, while God built a hell to roast his.

Again how foolish to teach that Christ had no place to lay his head, while the priesthood are forever

## THE STORY OF THE ZODIAC.

begging money to build magnificent temples, and the most of the people without homes.

The priesthood always lived on the fat of the land, from the contributions of the poor, and once through indulgences they sold to their dupes. How much better are they today?

As one Catholic put it: "It is a high mass for a rich man, a low mass for a poor man and no mass for a pauper."

I speak of the Catholic Church because it is the principal church. The Protestant churches were nothing but disgruntled factions or daughters of the old harlot, the Catholic church.

They quarreled over forms and ceremonies and not over just dealings.

Even the relics of the selected books they call the Bible, which were originally written by astrologers and just men who claim God, says in Revelations:

"The mother of harlots, I will make a bed for her and her children I will kill with death."

Remember the Bible, referring to the church, often speaks of it as a woman, as Christ is made to speak of the bride.

As all church forms are children of the Catholic church, of course she is the mother of harlots, and the Protestant church the daughters, and they all uphold interest on money and the schemes of the money mongers to rob the masses of the products of labor and of nature's gifts.

The Catholic church will be purged and cleansed and the truth taught once more and the Protestant churches will be killed, (i. e.) disbanded. Creeds and forms will have no place. Even the Catholic church will become the corner-stone of Socialism, and the golden rule will be made possible, and one man's rights will cease where another man's rights begin.

You ask, "In what way have they played the harlot?"

## THE STORY OF THE ZODIAC.

Have they not talked of the golden rule and justice to all, and bitterly opposed interest on money, and then yielded to the privileged classes and submitted to all of the robbers' systems, practiced by the privileged classes.

No poor man feels at home in the magnificent temples among the gorgeously arrayed, and so church attendance is dropping off, and the church is looked upon as a rich man's club room.

It their heaven has its classes and its inequalities it will only be a place of strife, like this world.

The moral teachings of the Church or of Free Masonry are as beautiful today as they ever were.

With all of the supposed brotherly love of Masonry, are they not as hypocritical as the church? Is it not a rich man's club, supported by the small fry?

What are their degrees? The very name degree is taken from astrology, but through it they become an organization of classes, generally rated in dollars and cents, that it costs to become a member. Thus the church or Masonry do not make intellect and moral worth the standard of honor, but dollars and cents.

What nonsense to talk of virtues and then practice exclusiveness.

"We meet upon a level and part upon a square."

This is a pretty parting ceremony, but what a lie.

How can they meet upon a level when they are classed in degrees?

They say, "A man once a Mason is always a Mason."

A few years ago a friend of mine, a comrade and member of the Grand Army, was in hard luck and asked me to use my influence to get him a situation. I knew he had paid into Masonry and other orders hundreds of dollars, so I asked, "Why do you not call on the Masons and other orders to whom you have paid so much money; their influence must be a thousand-fold greater than mine?"

Said he, "I am not in good standing."

"Not in good standing," I cried. "What do you mean? I know you to be a good man, an honest man."

"Yes," said he. "But I am behind in my dues."

"Great Scott," I cried. "You did not need them when you were paying them this money, now you are without money, what good are they to you?"

The Grand Army remitted his dues and found him a job because he needed it. This is true brotherhood.

Let all men stop preaching the golden rule unless they are willing to try to bring it in universal practice.

When a Mason hinted he would like to take my name in to the lodge, I replied, "I do not think I have a right to join."

He did not ask me why and I suppose thought I was not eligible, but I do not believe in the degree system and could not be a hypocrite for the same reason I could not join the church, yet both offer beautiful teachings and of course must do some good and I have friends in all societies and I wish them no evil.

There is no longer any ground for the Church and Masonry to clash. They healed their differences when they got Morgan to write a book apparently exposing Masonry, that the world might know Modern Masonry is built on Church lines. Of course, to give color to this thing, it was supposed Morgan was killed by Masons, but all they gave to the world was for their advantage, for who could be opposed to their beautiful teachings? But the teaching of such things and the practicing something else is what I am opposed to.

Of course, there are many good and sincere people in both church and Masonry, and their intentions are

## THE STORY OF THE ZODIAC.

good, but it is the false teachings sugar-coated with beautiful moral precepts that I object to.

It is silly to talk of universal peace, when the great nations trample upon the rights of smaller ones, or to think that the invention of diabolical implements of destruction will stop war, where strife will merely change from open warfare to most horrible forms of secret assassination.

There is no necessity of a thousandth part of the laws we have to prohibit, and which do not prohibit. But our laws should be made to protect men in their rights or to find where any man's rights begin and to protect him in them.

We would give the little horse the long end of the evener, but with our fellow man we always give the advantage to the rich and powerful, or privileged class.

Let us try to establish a heaven for our brother here and teach him to do so for others, and we will do a thousand-fold more to prepare him for the world to come than we can by dinging into his ears a story of a world he must know we know no more of than he does.

There is no necessity for creeds, ceremonies and degrees to teach the golden rule, that one man's rights must cease where another man's rights begin.

Will Church people and Masons join hands with Socialism, of which government and municipal ownership is the first step, to make the practice of the golden rule possible? It is not possible, with our false systems, hence the individual is not to blame for practicing the false system, but is to blame for upholding it.

This does not mean that a donkey should be taken, as a companion, into the parlor of the refined man, or that the refined man should not receive enough to support a condition consistent with his refinement, but true refinement will be the standard and not vulgar desire for wealth and power and the right to de-

## THE STORY OF THE ZODIAC.

clare one's self a divine right to be king or to form false systems and trusts to rob his fellow man.

---

"If any man pull down the American flag shoot him on the spot," said John A. Dix. More noble words were never uttered by man.

Every now and then we hear of a gathering of Socialists insulting the American flag. Whenever such a thing takes place it is through the ignorance of a few foreigners, who were denied the right to plead for justice under the banners for which they were compelled to fight, and so were driven to adopt a flag, which was the red flag, because it was supposed to typify the blood that flows in all men's veins alike. They never seem to think that vile, selfish men will "steal the livery of heaven to serve the devil," that their own flag has become the emblem of rottenness, that it is the auctioneer's emblem, that it is a most fitting emblem for labor organizations for hundreds of years, because the laboring class have never been true to themselves, forever selling out their brothers whenever opportunity afforded. They often force employers to be hard because of their own selfishness and dishonesty.

Nothing would please the enemies of a reform movement better than to have its supporters insult the American flag. If furnishes them just the weapon they want, and their paid tools are the very ones to lead the poor fools on.

Science and reason teaches us there is an intelligent creative principle, call it God or what you will. Evolution is a law of that power. The American flag is a product of fthat law. It is a God given emblem, an emblem of all that is good. The blue field and white stars in our flag is an emblem of the canopy of heaven, that shelters all alike, the rich and the poor, that gives to the weak the right to combine, in defense of justice, against the unprincipled strong.

### THE STORY OF THE ZODIAC.

The white in our flag is an emblem of purity, to remind you that without purity of purpose and faithful adehrence to your cause nothing can be gained.

The red in our flag embodies all that the most fastidious mind could ever see in the red flag of the Commune.

The stripes in our flag represent the stripes the vigilant must war who protect its beautiful folds.

O! ye men, who call yourselves reformers, how can you insult this God given banner?

It is true it has been disgraced by selfish, unprincipled men, but so has every other emblem of justice. Had you followed that flag through the smoke of battle, as I have, to abolish chattel slaver that wage slavery might next be abolished, you would never insult it. Let me say, if any man insult the American flag, set him down for a fool or an enemy to humanity.

The South was wrong, but had she clung to the stars and stripes as her heritage, and seized the capital, it is a question whether the North ever would have defeated her.

Ye reformers, above all things cling to the flag. It is your flag, and this country is your country. It is the only country that has given a man a fighting chance to win his liberty, from the enthrallment of selfishness and greed.

It is true dishonest men have stolen your money and, still worse, have stolen your votes, aye your very senses, and you may yet have to fight for your rights as they are doing in Russia; but such a thing is not yet necessary and let us hope never will be, for in this country successful men seem to be more willing to listen to reason, and we have had some noble men at the head of our nation, men who were friends of honest toil and not the upholders of greed.

Washington was a very rich man, but he refused to be a king, and his motto was "Equality and the Fatherhood of God."

## THE STORY OF THE ZODIAC.

The motto of the noble Lincoln was "Justice before the law and the brotherhood of man."

Jackson was a well-known friend of labor; his motto was "Legislate for the producer, the rich can take care of themselves."

Jefferson's motto was "Equal rights to all and privileges to none."

Our good President Roosevelt is doing for humanity all that any man can do. True he may make mistakes, for it is human to err every man makes mistakes, but we would show our appreciation for what he does. Ingratitude is one of the greatest failings any man can be cursed with.

Masonry does not pretend to be anything else but a selfish organization, asks no one to become a member, and protects its organization by absolute refusal to discuss Masonry. All we can find fault with is that all secret organizations are inimical to good government and the final brotherhood of man. This is also applicable to religious denominations or societies. It is perfectly natural for any man to be biased in favor of his lodge or church brother. Corrupt men know this and use these organizations as stepping stones to power. It is useless to deny this to any observing man. In all such organizations the small fry are barely tolerated as supporters of ambitious men.

The religious bodies are many times worse than secret societies, because their very acts show their foundation and their conduct falsifies their claims. They start out by presenting to us a mutilated book, which they know little or nothing about. If they knew anything about it why did they quarrel and murder thousands because they could not believe just thus and so? Finally settling on two versions of this old Astrological work that they do not understand, and most of them are afraid to discuss hon-

### THE STORY OF THE ZODIAC.

estly, they try to drive off honest discussion by the story of a terrible punishment if you lose your faith in their idea of a God, who they say is the author of this very much mutilated book which they do not understand. According to their version, they make that God a monster worse than the vilest savage of his creation. They mistake an allegorical character for a real character. This, however, is not so bad if they were not a stumbling block to human progress, by opposing the use of the reasoning faculties nature's God has given us. This is not all. They have their nose in everybody's business. Not only this, but if they were not divided among themselves they would retard the educational progress of our children, by forcing their teaching in our public schools, thus taking the time that should be given to other studies.

Not only this, but they make false claims, pretending the church is the foundation of all civilization, when in fact civilization has come up in spite of the church, she being the favored of all trusts, going scot free of all taxation. Her boasted building of morals is refuted by the number of criminal preachers, of whom one authority places at twenty per cent, and business men generally prefer to trust a man who makes no prtensions to religion than one who makes such a profession.

I do not wish to offend the good and conscientious church people, for they have as much right to their belief as I or anyone else have to theirs, and no more. But to prove what I say, here are the headings of what I find in this very day's paper, March 11, 1907:

"Secret political church society at Grand Rapids will oppose all candidates of liberal ideas."

"A school teacher, near Jackson, Mich., invited a Protestant minister to read from the Bible and offer prayers, whereupon Mr. Bruer, a Catholic, threatens to take his children out of school, and if he does he is liable to be arrested."

## THE STORY OF THE ZODIAC.

"Prof. Briggs is advocating a 'constitutional Papacy' and the reorganization of the Roman Catholic Church on the lines that have worked so well in political institutions."

All students of history should remember how well it worked in Constantine's time. When the Pagan church was going down and the young Christian church coming up, the Pagan church pretended to accept the new doctrine, but quickly went back to her old false teachings, but under the new name and the money-devil power the whole lot are supporting today.

"At the Pastors' Union the preachers have a rumpus over the Anti-Canteen Report." The officers of the army, who should know best, have decided that the canteen is a decided benefit to the men, but these overwise preachers must stick their noses in the matter. They "Strain at a gnat and swallow a camel." Do you hear them hotly speak of the lost souls, the dwarfed minds and bodies of thousands of children, driven by poverty to work in factories, or of the 500,000 annual casualties, mostly the result of greed? I guess not. Why? ? ?

## JUPITER.

Is 380,000,000 miles from sun and 91,000 miles in diameter.

## THE ASTROLOGERS BELIEF OR CREED, AND WHY HE DOS OR DOES NOT BELIEVE.

But, first what the astrologer does not believe. As faith or belief is not a thing of voluntary action, it must be hypocritical to pretend to believe what is inconsistent to a mind not constituted to believe that thing desired, hence we do not believe salvation depends on faith or belief. But we do believe the promise of a heavenly mansion to the believer, or an everlasting torment to the non-believer was a promise on the one hand and a threat on the other, to keep a following together to support a sleek and lazy priesthood, in idleness and luxury, we are charitable enough to believe that has but little weight at present.

The Astrologer believes the universe is made up of intelligent atoms; this constitutes the whole, we call God. These atoms are continually forming organic bodies, under given laws; we call the laws of nature. The intelligence of these organic bodies depends, upon the plane they are on, and upon the personal efforts each individual organic body makes to rise. This necessitates the law of evolution, and of reincarnation. Any one can see the tendency of all nature is upward through construction of the molecules; this necessitates, to some extent, self-independence, which itself is under a process of cultivation, though always subject to natural law.

We believe by bad conduct and bad associations we hinder progress and cause suffering we will regret. On the other hand, we believe that by prayer and by persistent effort we attract to us the finer elements and increase our progress.

We admit self-sacrifice is the highest form of kindly generosity, yet we cannot believe that where a human judge could not be found who would let an innocent man die for the guilty, or that would admit such a thing could benefit the guilty, only as a reformer's self-sacrifice is an example to others, we believe God would not act less humane or less wise than a human judge, though the present christian teaching is to the contrary.

The Astrologer believes in one supreme God, or universal intelligence, as stated in Isaiah xliv., 6: "I am the first, and I am the last; and beside me there is no God."

We believe this because—

"We hear Thee in the insect's hum,
And in the bird's sweet warbling song;
We hear Thee in old ocean's moan,
And in the rolling thunder's tone.
All things around proclaim aloud
An omnipresent living God.
If universal, we presume
For ought but thee, there is no room."

Psalms cxxxix., 6 to 9:

"Whither shall I go from thy spirit? or whither shall I flee from thy presence?

"If I ascend up into heaven, thou art there; if I make my bed in hell, behold, thou art there.

"If I take the wings of the morning, and dwell in the uttermost parts of the sea; even there shall thy hand lead me, and thy right hand shall hold me."

We believe all men are the sons of God, because he is the author of all things.

We believe the ideal character of Christ the most perfect that man ever conceived of, and that it is beneath the dignity of any person to let the admiration of that character or the following of the precept attributed to him, to rest upon the possible existence or manner of begetting such a being.

## THE STORY OF THE ZODIAC.

We believe the Christian Bible contains many good things, but that it is the work of man. To claim it directly the work of God, is to insult that great intelligence.

If a man tells us two conflicting stories we will not believe him. Then why should we acept as truth the conflicting stories we find in a book, of which we have no records or proofs of the dates of its creation?

We give a few instances here, not to wantonly offend anyone, but to substantiate our position, and show to the world we are careful searchers after turth.

Exodus xxxiii., 11: "And the Lord spake unto Moses face to face, as a man speaketh unto his friend."

As a man speaketh to a friend face to face, is to see him.

In the same chapter, 20th verse: "And he said. Thou canst not see my face; for there shall no man see me, and live."

If such a square contradiction was found in any other book no man would attempt to defend it; but in the Bible, the very presentation of a possible contradiction is apt to find condemnation.

Now let us take II. Chronicles, xxi., 5: "Jehoram was thirty and two years old when he began to reign, and he reigned eight years in Jerusalem."

And the 20th verse says he departed.

The second verse of the following chapter says Ahaziah, his youngest son, took his place, and he was forty and two years when he began to reign.

As the father was only forty when he died, the son must be two years older than his father.

Would the God of the universe have made two such blunders?

Now read Matthew. 1st chapter, and compare it with Luke iii., and you will see there are two distinct lineages for Christ, who it is claimed was a direct

## THE STORY OF THE ZODIAC.

descendant from the seed of David, through Mary—not Joseph—and yet such a descent must come through the male.

Now look at the contradiction of the story of Judas, the betrayor of Christ. Matthew XXVII-5 says, "And he cast down the pieces of silver in the temple and went out and hanged himself."

Then in Acts, 1-18, says, "Now this man purchased a field, with the reward of iniquity and falling headlong, he burst asunder in the midst, and all his bowels gushed out." See explanation on page 135 of "Bible Astrology."

Such errors are on a parallel with similar errors made by story writers of today, hence we judge the Bible the work of man, but a very valuable book to read.

These are but few of many such things that can be pointed out to prove the Bible the work of man.

The object of the pointing out of these things is to show the God of the universe would naturally place his records on more substantial foundation than the changeable, perishable works of man     . hence the astrologer turns to the everlasting stars, for God's record, and proves it was what astrologers of ancient times found there and is what he was writing of in the Bible, though his records have been sadly twisted by religious fanatics.

The astrologer sees in the Bible the records of the great men of his craft, and he uses it as an aid to unravel the mystery of nature and nature's God.

The astrologer believes progress is God's law, because he sees the tendency of all things is upward.

The vine crawls upward to heat and light, the lower animals aspire to the companionship of man, except those who fear him. Man aspires to a home with God.

Where cultivation is found there all nature makes the most rapid progress, except where that cultivation is tied to old forms. The grass that feels the sharp-tooth rake grows better than that which is neglected.

The fruit tree that feels the pruning hook makes greater progress than that which does not. The steel is brightened by friction. The human mind is brightened by experience. For these reasons we believe in evolution, and we believe that reincarnation is a necessity to intelligent results of evolution.

The astrologer believes man always did exist in some form and always will exist, and that experience of pain is necessary to the enjoyment of pleasure; therefore he cannot believe in eternal hell or eternal heaven, as the latter would become monotonous and intolerable, and hell become bearable, and possibly enjoyable, from familiarity. Besides it would make God a cruel revengeful God.

Besides to burn so as to give pain is to disintegrate, to consume. If it does not do that it does not give pain, and if it does destroy, then it is not eternal, hence an everlasting hell is a deception to scare children and the weak minded, while the law of compensation, is a logical conclusion from cause and effect.

The astrologer does not believe in continual progress without intermission as it is not consistent with nature. The night is a rest to the day. The winter is a rest to the summer. The elementary state is a rest between compound conditions of the elements, and we believe a spirit state is a place of rest between incarnated lives. A place where we know all things and review our past lives and prepare for the next. That we may try to avoid the mistakes of this life.

It would be as foolish to take one's work bench to bed with him as to think of progress in the spirit state.

Though the spirit of a departed friend, is with the fountain head and knows all things, when called back, he can only come back in the point of knowledge he possessed when he left us.

The astrologer believes in spirit communication, and because of the diversity of forms of intelligence the right to any religious belief should be tolerated, so long as it does not infringe on the rights of another to an unbearable state, or to the injury and the hindrance of progress of the community.

A wise man recently said in the United States senate.

### AFRAID OF FREEDOM.

Here is an utterance of rare wisdom. It is from a recent speech by Senator John Sharp Williams, and is one of the finest and truest things ever said: "My friends, men in religion, men in trades, men in politics, have been afraid of freedom ever since the world began. God Almighty seems to be the only being anywhere who is not afraid of freedom, and not afraid to give it to his creatures. He gives it to such an extent that he lets us go wrong if we will—even to that extent. From the beginning religious bigots have been afraid of it, political bigots have been afraid of it, and industrial bigots have been afraid of it. And yet, whenever it comes, we find it stimulates human enterprise, human industry and human intelligence to such an extent that it more than compensates for what seem to be the plain and palpable and obvious immediate losses by it.—Boston Times.

The astrologer believes that a religion that is unjust, and injurious to the people of this world, is an enemy to God and a hindrance to progress and the enjoyment of another world; therefore we believe it is wrong to pretend to save men from a hell in another world while doing nothing to save them from hell in this world.

The astrologer believes, if a man wrongs another in this world, he must suffer a similar wrong in his next incarnated life; if he strives to benefit others, others will strive to benefit him in another life; hence—

## THE STORY OF THE ZODIAC.

"Whatsoever ye do unto others, it shall be meted out unto you."

"An eye for an eye, and a tooth for a tooth."

Such was the old law, and it is said, "Christ came not to change one jot or tittle of the old law."

The astrologer believes in the Golden Rule: "Do unto others as ye would have others do unto you."

The astrologer would render the Ten Commandments as follows, that they might be better understood:

1. "Thou shalt have no other Gods before me." Because a universal God leaves no room for any other God. To bow down before any other part or thing is to divide the attention from the true God, and to lead to selfish ends.

2. "Thou shalt not take the name of the Lord thy God in vain." Nor shalt thou use any idle and foolish language, because it corrupts speech, and hinders thy progress and the progress of others by cumbering society with useless and unseemly things.

3. "Six days shalt thou labor and do all thy work." Because God hath set us the example, and in all nature teaches us there is a time to work and a time to rest, and a time for all things, and we should not deprive even our own bodies of proper and regular rest, because our bodies are made up of many intelligent parts, that we may wish to call to us again, but will keep from us and hinder our progress because we have been hard taskmasters.

4. Thou shalt religiously keep this in view, as a day of rest, not of extra labor for the servants, that you may indulge thy pleasures, to the detriment of others and to thine own body.

5. "Honor thy father and thy mother, that their days may be long with thee." And that thy children and thy children's children may honor and love thee, and thy posterity be a blessing in the land.

## THE STORY OF THE ZODIAC.

6. "Thou shalt not kill." Because thou canst not restore life, and to wrong another thou wrongest thy God and thyself and add woe to all things.

7. "Thou shalt not commit adultery." Because in so doing thou breakest thy pledges and cause others to break pledges, and lower society by disrespecting the laws of God and man.

8. "Thou shalt not steal." Neither by stealth, nor by law, nor by custom, nor by any way that taketh an advantage of thy brother; for by so doing you break the golden rule, while pretending to obey God's laws, and are thereby worse than the thief at night.

9. "Thou shalt not bear false witness against thy neighbor." Either directly or by inference, or assassinate his character because he is not of thy creed, party, politics, or social standing; for thou hast no greater rights than another, and to assume such rights thou becomest a thief and a robber, and an assassinator of character.

10. "Thou shalt not covet anything that is thy neighbor's." Because it leads to selfishness and dishonesty and to all that is filthy and wrong.

11th. This is the commandment said to be given by Christ. "Love one another, and love thy neighbor as thyself." Do this and it covers all of the commandments.

This life must have been for a purpose.

If there is not a recompense for every pang of pain or sorrow, from the tearing to pieces of the least molecule to the mightiest organic body, life in this world is to no purpose; hence eternal hell or eternal death that brings oblivion must mean a purposeless life on earth, if God knows all things.

We should not charge God with cruelties we condemn men for committing.

We have outlived the cruelties of past ages, hence have outlived the misunderstanding and mistranslation and mistakes in the Bible, to longer teach such things is to hinder progress.

# THE EVOLUTION OF THE BIBLE.

I cannot refrain quoting a little Biblical history in support of the facts I have before recorded.

I first quote from "The Life of Jehoshua," by Dr. Franz Hartman.

Kant regarded Christ as an ideal human perfection.

John Steward Mill, as a very extraordinary man.

Lord Amberly, as an iconoclastic idealist.

Ficht as the first teacher who revealed the unity of man with supreme spirit.

Hagel as "an incarnation of the Logos."

Schilling, as a kind of Avator (ie) one of the periodical decents of the Divinity.

Let me here say these periodical descents were merely the periodical return of the allegorical story of the son's annual appearant trip through the Zodiac as given in this work.

Dr. Keim supposed Christ to be merely a mysterious man, whose glorified spirit inspired his deciples to attempt the reformation of the world. Something like Mrs. Eddie or the late Elisha Dowie and many others.

Strauss looked upon Christ as a moral reformer, who occasionally stooped to imposture to secure the confidence of his followers.

Renan, as an effeminate idealist, an impcstor who performed bogus phenomona.  .

Schleiermacher, as a man in whom self confidence. was so saturated with the divine principle, that he really became a God incarnate.

Antole Brmbe, as a modern anarchist and socolist of the most firey kind.

Gerold Massey, who bases his opinion upon historical researches, finds that Jehoshua Ben-Pandera

## THE EVOLUTION OF THE BIBLE.

was born some 120 years before our Christian eria, and that the typical Christ of the Gospels was made up from the features of various Gods."

None of the above wise men from whom these quotations were taken were astrologers, or they would have seen all stories of a mesiah were drawn from the same source, i. e., the allegory of the annual trip of the Sun and planets. The searcher after truth should look to the opinions of disinterested persons and not from that class alone whose occupation or self interests would blind their eyes to but one side of the subject.

It is not the object of this work to hinder or tare down an element of reform but to establish truth.

A false basis or false premises either are a bad foundation to establish or base morals upon.

The example set by the ideal character of Christ can be just as well taught and followed, if the truth is known or sought and proven to be an ideal character, as it can be if a true character, and those who pretend to love the truth should be the first to desire it to be proven, and they should glory in the evidence that shows such an allegory to be found in the movements of the heavenly bodies.

I have no desire to change the ideal character or spiritual side of those books of the Bible which were written by those old astrologers and the Christian who claims to love the truth should be pleased to know any person loves the truth to the extent of delving in forgotten lore in search of it. This book need not interfere with the pure work of Christianity as it was written in the interest of truth.

No great and lasting good can be established under an absolute lie. The deception must be found out sooner or later.

After reading "Stowe's Bible Astrology" the read-

## THE EVOLUTION OF THE BIBLE.

er must conclude—the old testament was chiefly the work of astrologers who sought this method to preserve the history of the world, as well as to fortell its future to the Sun's passage into Sagittarius, when the history will again be repeated. These astrologers knew, their work must be interpreted by the wise men of the future (ie) the astrologers, who were called wise men, in their day.

The new testament was written as an allegory on the annual appearant motion of the Sun, Moon and Stars, which was the basis of Sun worship, which looked upon the Sun as the visible representative of the great creative principle, hence the Sun of God.

I have given Also another story pictured in the old testament of Uranus as the Son of the Sun God, which must not be confounded with the above.

The new testament was written to show what should be rather than what was, or as a beacon light to lead man on to a better life.

There is plenty of evidence that not one of the books of the new testament were written until 150 years after the supposed birth of Christ, and nobody knows who wrote them. These books are full of contradictions and errors. For instance the Gospel of John says that Bethsaida was in Galilee, while there is no such town in the district and never was.

Bethsaida, says Potter's Bible encyclopedia, was on the east side of the sea of Tiberias, where as Galilee was on the west side, would John not know where his own birth place was, as it is said he was born at Bethsaida; and if he wrote the book, would he have made such a mistake?

The amount of it is the priesthood were then making their living by preaching to the people as they are doing today, and in seeking for authority they gathered these books for text books as our school teachers use certain text books to day, and they

## THE EVOLUTION OF THE BIBLE

gathered all kinds of books, astrological works, histories, good and bad, and allegories. It is a historical fact that at least one priest had in his canon, Josephus, Esoph's Fables and other similar books.

When the priests got to quarreling about which books were the proper books to be used, they on more than one occasion threw out the books of Daniel and Revelation. These books are astrological and their prophesies are much extold by the preachers of today.

Says Bronson C. Keeler in a work entitled "A short history of the Bible," published in 1888:

"When the Catholic Church began to be formed, about the year 170-180 A. D., the tendency was to use fewer books, and the ones accepted as authoritative began to be called divine."

The Bible is no more sacred than any other book and no more inspired than other books, for if the God of the universe stooped to so small a thing as the authorship of such a book he would never have left it to poor weak man to blunder over in selections, translations and interpretation. In my "Agnostic's Lament," I have given the names of 23 books the Bible speaks of which were left out of it.

In that little work I also point out many contradictions and erors. The book also contains three of as fine poems as ever written. ( price 10 cents. )

Says Mr. Keeler: "The first collection of New Testament books ever made was by Marcion, about the year 145 A. D. It consisted of one Gospel and ten of Paul's Epistles, and they were not then considered the word of God."

The first old Testament list was by Melito, bishop of Sardis, about 175 A. D."

Mr. Keeler then gives the dates and places where bishops and priests selected the books they thought

## THE EVOLUTION OF THE BIBLE.

best, and gives the dates of their quarrels until they finally met in councils at different places to select their books, the first council was held 393 A. D. at Hippo, in Africa. In 419 A. D. another council was held at Carthage and in 431 A. D., a third council was held at Ephesus. By this time the disputes as to which books should be used had assumed factional fighting phases and both sides came to this council armed and were more disorderly than were our old political conventions and their brutish orgies compelled the authorities to patrol the streets with troops to keep order.

Mr. Keeler quotes from many authors to show the priesthood were but an ignorant rabble whose understanding of the books was so mixed, that they got the titles of books confounded. There met another council at Ephesus in 449. This was conducted so shamefully that one priest struck another and the friends of the assailing priest, like a pack of wolves, fell upon the fallen man and kicked him to death," says Mr. Keeler, and he gives authority.

"Another council, called to meet in Nicea in 451 A. D., which was so unruly that it had to be summoned to Chaledea, across the straits from Constantinople, where the 'Emperor could reach it with his troops and compell orde.r

"Another council, held at Constantinople in 785 A. D., the soldiery burst into the chamber and dispersed the affrighted bishops because they did not approve of the bishops' enactments and the second council of Nicea (787 A. D.) denounced this council of Constantinople as a synod of fools and mad men."

Henry L, Count of Champagne, (1165 A. D.), wrote to John of Salisbury, secretary to Thomas A. Becket, asking him how many books there really were in the Bible, and who were their authors." This shows how "little was known of the Bible."

## THE EVOLUTION OF THE BIBLE.

To show how little the leading church men or bishops knew of the books they were fighting about in (1318 A. D.), a Nestorian bishop gave a list of what he supposed were "divine books" in the old Testament he included Ecclesiasticus the wisdom of Solomon, Judith, the Story of Susanna, the Lesser Daniel and Baruch, which, later books are not now in the Bible, he also adds the books of Traditions of the Elders (the Mishna), the works of Josephus, the fables of Esoph, the history of the Son's Samonas, the books of Maccabees, the history of King Herod, the book of Last Desolation, of Jerusalem by Titus, Asiatha, wife of Joseph, the Just son of Jacob, and the book of Tobias and Tobit, not seeming to know the two last mentioned, were one and the same. Here he excluded several books now in the Bible. He seemed to have no idea of the Bible as we now know it."

"In 1441 a council at Florence adopted the list which the council of Trent subsequently reiterated.

"The council of Trent met Dec. 13-1545 and on Feb. 12-1546, the question of the cannon was brought forward. Luther had declared that the Bible alone was the source of authority. The church declared tradition to be of equal authority. Luther declared that the universally accepted books of the Old and New Ttestament, without any of the apocrypha be admitted. The questions were discussed in the council by about thirty ecclesiastics in four sessions. For the second time in the history of the book came a compromise. Four factions were contending for the adoption of different views. All were agreed that tradition—hearsay, rumor—was of equal authority with written records."

Here was the dividing of the ways between the Catholic and Protestants and two different Bibles chosen. Here were the real opening guns that deluged the world in blood.

## THE EVOLUTION OF THE BIBLE.

"In 1827 the British and Foreign Bible societies decided they would no longer circulate the books of the Apocrypha. The American Bible Society followed its example, and thus it was that our Bible received its finishing touch, as we have been accustomed to see it. Except as it was recently patched up by the new translation. About that time the following cablegram was received from London, where the revision took place:

"A new revision of the Bible has just been completed, including the apocryha, upon which the revisers have been engaged since 1881, and it will shortly be issued from the Oxford Press in various sizes, uniform with the revised Old and New Testament."

It is not a revision of the Bible that is needed. A new translation is demanded. The so called King James translation, if not a fraud of itself, as some scholars contend, was not a translation, but a revision, as every reader can see by comparing it with the Bishop's Bible, which of itself was a revision of a still earlier revision. The first rendering, and that from the Latin Vulgate, has been the base of every subsequent pretended translation. The Catholic English Bible followed closely along the lines of King James' revision, and so with the Jewish pretended translation of the Old Testament. So difficult is it to understand the original, and give it an honest rendering into English, a late writer who seems to know whereof he is discoursing says:

"If ten Greek scholars were given certain well-known texts in the Greek New Testament, and were instructed to give their own renderings, each ignorant of former translations, there would be ten different renderings—in many respects conveying entirely different ideas."

And this is the reason for the multiplicity of revisions, and the avoidance of translations.

## THE EVOLUTION OF THE BIBLE.

"Let it be remembered the books of the Bible were not divided into chapters or punctuated, or even divided into words, but rantogether like this:

"Godsolovedtheworldthathegavehisonlybegottenson, and so forth."

If the reader looks back to the class of men who selected the books of the Bible and kicked out what they did not want, he may also understand they interpretated and placed in chapters which they did want. He may also understand these men were inferior in intelligence to the average of the American, English, German or French working man of to-day. But as Mr. Keeler says in his short Bible History:

"The origin of the books having been forgotten, men, credulous and in trouble, came to think that because the books were written of God they were writen by God. The reformers declared that the Bible and not the church was the sole source of authority. This succeeded, and the thunders of the Vatican were answered by the thunders of artillery. Armies swept across the face of Europe, and it was amid the roar of cannon, the shock of battle, and the shrieks of the dying, that the doctrine of the divine and infallible inspiration of the Bible grew."

Oh! Religion, what cruelties and wrongs have been perpetrated in thy name!

How such great questions, as to the authorship of books, their true meanings, or the destiny of man in a future state, could be decided by the vote of men who depended upon the church for a living, whose financial interests would lead them to decide according to their personal views, whose passions, the court records of today show are in no better state of control than that of the average man, no one has ever thought to discuss.

Here is still a greater curiosity. These men calling themselves the chosen of God, oppose every

## THE EVOLUTION OF THE BIBLE.

step in true reform, bitterly oppose spiritualism, reincarnation, and evolution, and then declare a book
infallible that they must know is an evolved work.
It is certainly amusing to the true student, if it had
not been a tragedy, but they had better stop now
b efore it becomes a farce.

The priesthood must have better opportunities for
gathering the truth than I have, which shows they
willingly stand a stumbling block to mental progress, because of bigotry and superstition, or because of financial interests, such as I have shown,
must be the interest of the Pope in opposing socialism. No discussion of the Bible can be entered into
properly which does not take this into consideration.

The church is not a natural reforming element,
but it's a mere money seeking institution, as shown
by the fact that it is always found where its financial
interests are the greatest, as was the case during
the American rebellion; the church divided without
a protest. Its excuse that it deals with the spiritual
only, is a mere subterfuge. As a sky pilot it shows
it knows nothing of the truth or it would not be
divided into a thousand factions.

In the face of the following extract from an article
in the Detroit News-Tribune of the date of April 21,
1907, it seems clear the church is a mere money-
grabbing institution, and opposes everything that
does not bring money into its coffers:

"Wealth owned by the Trinity church, New York,
$165,000,000. Annual income at 6 per cent, $1,200,000.
It owns and rents property for business purposes,
offices, and even saloons. This vast property is han-
dled by such men as those whose names were made
familiar in the recent life insurance and campaign
fund investigations, and who are connected actively

## THE EVOLUTION OF THE BIBLE..

with New York trust companies. Edmund D. Randolph, senior vestryman of the church, as treasurer of the New York Life Insurance Company, signed the $48,702.50 checks to reimburse George W. Perkins for his contribution to the Republican national committee, and the details of certain of his syndicate transactions are to be found in the printed testimony of the Armstrong committee."

This is a vast untaxed property of but one church organization whose income may be used to shape legislation to their satisfaction.

These vast values of untaxed church property are evidence of a protected trust which is dangerous to the interests and welfare of the people, and a menace to justice, equality and liberty.

The very best and strongest feature of the Bible is it condemnation of interest on money. "Take thou no usury or increase." According to Ezekiel the Jews were scattered because they took usury and greedily gained one of another, and the Bible tells them Christ drove the money changers from the temple, yet they uphold the money changer and rent property to saloons for gain, while they howl against the sale of liquor.

Of course I will be accused of infidelity and, if possible, railroaded to hades. I will certainly be accused of desiring to lower the morals of my fellowman, which would be false; but I do say you cannot purify a roily stream at its mouth—you must go to its source—and the church is forever pointing at the slums, but seldom saying a word against the rot of the leaders of society. Look to the magnificent gifts of those leaders to the Pope and churches, and

## THE EVOLUTION OF THE BIBLE.

every divine expects a percentage from everything he buys, which he must know is added on to the price of the goods others have to buy, also millions of church property untaxed, and you need not ask the reason why.

I do not deny the existence of a supreme being, because scientifically I trace his intelligence from the wisest man to the least atom, and prove not by the votes of self-interested, passion-racked brains, but by science, comparison and reason, that Evolution and re-incarnation are natural laws and stepping stones to a higher life; that the man who associates with dogs or criminals will suffer in such degraded lives, as will also the man who preaches hell will for a time suffer hell, until both evolve out of their conditions in future lives. As must also the millionaire who knows he is taking more than his share of the products of labor, go to the very dregs of the next social world and wonder why he has such bad luck, just as many of us are doing today. Nor will a few gifts to the church, to deceive the poor, or to a college to educate the sons of the rich, help them out of it, especially when they know they intend to raise the price of oil, iron or other commodities to get the money back from the consumer, or to get it back by interest on money.

Is it not clear that religion was evolved, that the Bible was evolved, and is it not consistent with the fact that man was evolved, and can be seen in his mechanical products of today?

Evolution is a natural law that no observant, unprejudiced mind can deny, then as we cannot account for the expression of thought without universal mind. As we recognize some minds greater than others, in organic form we must admit of a great organic mind who ordained the evolution of man and the evolution of the Bible.

More than eight years after the foregoing quotations were first read, or January 28, 1898, I penned

## THE EVOLUTION OF THE BIBLE.

the following. Having the future foretold me in detail, and names of people mentioned who wouold come into my life and who did so, years after, of people I knew nothing of and of events which could not have been by accident or prearranged by any man, but which show positive evidence to me, that I am influenced by destiny, which by right doing I can in a measure overcome. Yet any experience I may have had would be no evidence to one who never had such an experience.

If I have a destiny there is a destiner or supreme being, and I must live again whether I want to or not; then so far as I can I must help the law of evolution. I must reach down to draw others up where I am; I must reach up to be drawn up to those above me, and this must be done on new grounds, as we have outlived the old and justice and equality of man's rights must be acknowledged. It is safer for the worldly great to give up peaceably than to kick against the pricks.

If any person thinks the church people are willing to take a step forward, let him try to get them into any discussion which will benefit man, and he will soon find they are wedded to their idols.

I tried it through the religious columns of the Sunday News-Tribune and found myself soon choked off; but they can't choke me off from publishing a book like this.

I have heard someone left a sum of money for the man who would write a true history of the Bible, and I am sure a truer history than this canot be writ ten, though one might be more extensive in explana tion.

It is the duty of any man who loves the truth to do all he can to extend the circulation of this book, for if past experience is any criterion to go by, the biggots and enemies of truth will go to great extremes to prevent its circulation.

## OUR MOTTO.

As no one knows anything about a future world, and after thousands of years of wrangling, disputing and fighting with no good results, we offer this motto.

One world at a time. Let us do all we can to perfect this world and we shall be fit candidates for another world, if there is one.

No influence of church or society shall weigh a farthing between it and justice.

We will fearlessly condemn error wherever we find it, but with toleration.

Let us reach down and draw others up where we are and reach up to be drawn up to those above us.

Our flag, the Stars and Stripes. Our country, we will labor to purify it, to the end that we may have "Equal Opportunities for All and Special Privileges to None." The man who is opposed to this at once admits he is opposed to a square deal.

The necessities of one man cannot be judged by the desires of another man.

It may require an engineer and a mule to build a railroad, but that does not justify the engineer in lowering the standard of his family, by taking the mule into his parlor.. Nor does it justify him in stealing the oats from the mule.

Our present grasping social system is a fit nursey for imps or offsprings of demons of a hell.

There is no fertilizer of selfishness or school of training for social corruption so far-reaching and corrupting in its influence as interest on money, yet one cannot live outside of social conditions; we take interest to avoid being consumed.

To destroy the cancer on the body politic the government alone must become the only money loaner.

There are eight million bank depositors, most of them small depositors. We are legal robbers, eighty-three millions without deposits.

If all were robbers there would be no one to rob.

Let us be honest with our God, with our posterity, with ourselves, and stop this robber system.

## THE ALLEGORY OF THE PRODIGAL SON.

So far I have only dealt with the straight forward story of the spiritual part of the Bible, and did not care to mix into that, many of the illogical and unreasonable things, or to point out contradictions and mistakes, for in this work I do not seek to belittle or tear down the spiritual side of the Bible, but to make its meaning plain, yet, of course, I could not explain everything in one volume of this size, yet I feel I must explain one other allegory in proof of the fact that the whole work is allegory, based upon Astrology, except, of course, that part which is very contradictory and bad history.

The story of the Prodigal Son will answer for all other allegories, as it is based upon the movements of the Sun, the same as the story of the Son of God.

I have before mentioned that the Babylonians were well up in all branches of science, especially in Astrology and mathematics. Recent excavations on the old cite of Babylon has revealed much of this and I give here quotations from a well-known writer and investigator.

### WHY SIXTY SECONDS MAKE A MINUTE.

Why is our hour divided into sixty minutes, each minute into sixty seconds, etc? Simply and solely because in Babylonia there existed, by the side of the decimal system, the sexagesimal, which counted by sixties. Why that number should have been chosen is clear enough, and it speaks well for the practical sense of these ancient Babylonian merchants. There is no number which has so many divisors as 60. The Babylonians divided the sun's daily journey into twenty-four parasangs, or 720 stadia. Each parasang or hour was subdivided into

THE STORY OF THE ZODIAC CONTINUED.

sixty minutes. A parasang is about a German mile,
and Babylonian astronomers compared the progress
made by the sun during one hour at the time of the
equinox to the progress made by a good walker
during the same time, both accomplishing one parasang. The whole course of the sun during the
twenty-four equinoxtial hours was fixed at twenty-
four parasangs, or 720 stadia, or 360 degrees. The
system was handed on to the Greeks, and Hip-
parchus, the great Greek philosopher, who lived
about 150 B. C., introduced the Babylonian hour
into Europe. Ptolemy, who wrote about 150 A. D.,
and whose name still lives in that of the Ptolemanic
system of astronomy, gave still wider currency to
the Babylonian way of reckoning time. It was carried along on the quiet stream of traditional knowledge through the middle ages, and strange to say,
it sailed down safely over the Niagara of the French
revolution. For the French, when revolutionizing
weights, measures, coins and dates, and subjecting
all to the decimal system of reckoning, were induced
by some unexplained motive to respect our clocks
and watches, and allowed our dials to remain sexagesimal—that is, Babylonian—each hour consisting
of sixty minutes. Here you see again the wonderful
coherence of the world, and how wnat we call
knowledge is the result of an unbroken tradition of
a teaching descending from father to son. Not more
than about a hundred arms would reach from us to
the builders of the palaces of Babylon, and enable
us to shake hands with the founders of the oldest
pyramids and to thank them for what they have done
for us.—Max Muller, in the Fortnightly Review.

Let the reader here notice the clock dial and the
Zodiac are one. The Zodiac is a circle of 360 degrees
divided like the clock dial into 12 parts or degrees,
minutes and seconds, while the clock dial being circular is of 360 degrees, divides into 12 parts or hours,
minutes and seconds.

THE STORY OF THE ZODIAC CONTINUED.

The prophesies of Daniel of times, time and a half a time, refers to the same system: "Times 720, a time 360, a half a time 180." Add these together and you have 1,260 astrological years of 360 days each, as that was formerly the length of their year. Thus 60 is a handy divisor here.

## THE PRODIGAL SON, OR SUN.

The illustration here given shows the central figure of the cut is a clock dial standing noon at Washington, D. C., while the 8 small dials show the

## THE STORY OF THE ZODIAC CONTINUED.

time at the cities given: First, top, New York, 12 minutes after 12. The second, to the right, is Chicago, 18 minutes after 11 a. m. The third, to the right, is New Orleans, 8 minutes after 11 a. m. The fourth is San Francisco, Cal., which stands 3 minutes to 9 a. m. The fifth, direct at the bottom, is Vienna, Austria, which stands 15 minutes to 6 p. m. The sixth is Berlin time, 2 minutes to 6 p. m. The seventh is Paris time, 7 minutes after 6 p. m. The eighth is London, England, 10 minutes after 5 p. m.

Outside of this circle of dials gives the verses of the 49th Chapter of Genesis, which belongs to each sign of the Zodiac, as given by the supposed ages of Jacob's sons, (which is an allegory, the same as the Prodigal Son), starting with Rubin, the eldest, at Libra, and running to the right through Scorpio, Sagittarius and Capricornus, and finally ending with Benjamin, the youngest son, in Virgo, sandwiched at the right of Joseph and left of Rubin, according to that other allegorical story of Joseph in Egypt, who, with Rubin, became responsible to their father for Benjamin.

The two cuts following this article give the symbols of the Zodical signs and planets, as found engraved on the Pyramids and oblisks of Egypt, and temples of India, which antedate all other histories by thousands of years and which are the basis of all religion. The circle with the dot, the Sun and Sun worship or eternal life, a circle or endless.

The half circle, the Moon or spirit; the circle with the cross represents us on earth to bear the burdens or cross of experience, for even God could not know the difference between pain and pleasure if he never thought of the two opposites, and we could know nothing only by experience, hence this life is a life of experience, but the true meaning of the cross has been corrupted in the Christian religion, and experience considered something to dred, while we should rejoice and bear the burden with fortitude.

This is the real picture intended to be illustrated in the story of the Prodigal Son. As before stated,

## THE STORY OF THE ZODIAC CONTINUED.

the story is based upon the daily motion of the Sun, as does the story of Father, the Son and the Holy Ghost, and the Twelve Disciples, and all of this is found on your watch dial, as well as a good compass.

Now look at your watch dial on the first cut in this story. Notice 12 o'clock noon. At 12 o'clock the Sun has reached his highest position. Remember the Sun is merely the representative of the great Creator, or he is the Son of God. At 1 o'clock he has left his high position and becomes the Prodigal Sun; he holds up one finger in derision. At 2 o'clock he holds up two fingers. At 3 o'clock, 3 fingers. Now one I stands for 1 o'clock. II's for 2 o'clock. III's for 3 o'clock. Ninety-nine out of a hundred without looking at their watch or clock, which they notice many times a day, if you ask them what stands for 4 o'clock they will say IV. But, does it? No, but IIII's, or four fingers, because the Babylonians used the fingers as numerals to a great extent.

At 5 o'clock the Prodigal Son, or Sun, holds up the thumb and forefinger. This former a letter V, which stands for Vicarous fila die, visgarent Son of God, or messenger of God, which represents the Miter worn on the Pope's breast.

At 6 p. m. the Son starts back to his highest point, or to his meridian on the other side of the globe.

It is now the Father and Son, but here he begins to choose his disciples.

The V standing for one figure or the repentant son. The X or the cross is also one figure, as he represents the perfect man. Remember the Sun Worshipers when standing facing the east, back to the west, arms extended, forms a cross or perfect man resigned to the worship of the Sun of God, afterward the allegorical Son of God

Now the V with two II's stands for the first two disciples. 8 o'clock represented VIII, four more disciples. 9 o'clock is represented by IX, the IX this

## THE STORY OF THE ZODIAC CONTINUED.

makes nine disciples. 10 o'clock represented by the X makes ten disciples, and at 11 o'clock represented by the XI cross and I makes the twelves disciples, now you have reached 12 o'clock, represented by XII. The two, X and the two II's, which stands for Father, Son and Holy Ghost, so here you have the complete story of the Prodigal Son, or Sun, leaving the Father and coming back to his high position and the fatted calf. Also the Father and Son, the Father, Son and Holy Ghost, all on your watch dial.

Here is a good compass on your watch dial, when you can see the Sun, point the hour hand on the watch dial to the Sun and the south is exactly half way between the hour hand and the XII on the dial, count forward up to noon and backward after the Sun has passed the meridian. For instance, suppose that it is 8 o'clock a. m. Point the hour hand to the Sun and the figure 10 on the dial is exactly south, if 4 p. m. and the II on the watch is south.

Thus all watches are compasses and a compass can be made a perfect chronometer by erecting a cover or staff east, standing at a right angle upward from the dial of the compass now draw a string from the top of the angle to the bottom, representing the west, or 6 on the dial, and make the compass the center of a watch dial, and the shadow of the string will fall on the exact minute of sun time. Thus your compass is an exact chronometer when the sun shines. This proves Astrology is the basis of the sun dial and finally your clock dial. The figure XII on the watch dial should be at the east, the IV at west, of course.

RIGHT HOURS TO SUCCESS.

THE HOUR DIAL TO GET THE RIGHT
HOURS FOR THE RIGHT BUSINESS OR OTHER
AFFAIRS THAT SURELY LEADS TO SUCCESS

## ASTROLOGY AS A SCIENCE.

ASTROLOGY AS A SCIENCE is the Mother of all sciences. It is the deepest, the most profound, and, if thoroughly understood, the most beneficial of all sciences. Yet there are educated bigots and ape-like followers who declare it to be an exploded theory, but they have never told us who exploded it. This is largely due to the would-be wit thrown at astrology, or the predictions of astrology by the press. This has caused many to suppose astrology is a superstition or a fake game of fortune tellers, and that no intelligent, self-respecting person would engage in it; and still, with this usage from the press, they wonder why we do not advertise more.

To get the truth before the public in a proper manner and free from contemptuous slur, we have been compelled, at great expense, to publish magazines and pamphlets. It is true that there are fake astrologers, as there are fakes in everything, and the greatest advertiser in anything is, generally, the greatest fake; because the enormous advertising bills must be paid by hook or by crook. An honest astrologer could not do work enough to pay such enormous bills, if he got the work to do. My work has brought me all the work I can do, without advertising, except the little I do in my book announcements. Even at a dollar, no man can get rich casting horoscopes. I do more writing than any lawyer would do for ten dollars. This is to say nothing of the mathematical labor or the stationery necessary.

Astrology is a science that few can understand and practice successfully, and is generally followed by old men, and more often than otherwise they are investigators and literary people and do not practice to any great extent, or if they do it is more in the interest of study than for the money there is in it.

It is true astrologers make mistakes, but no more than do other professionals. "It is human to err."

Professor Chaney, who died in Chicago in 1903, was 82 years old. Way back in 1877 he predicted his own death and that it would take place at the

## ASTROLOGY AS A SCIENCE.

age of 82, and that a tempest would be raging at the time. All of which took place.

Dr. Broughton, of New York, who died six years ago, was upward of seventy.

The late Ernest S. Green, of California, was nearing the 80 mark when he died.

Professor Hatfield was known so long in the astrological world as to stamp him as an old man.

Professor Loren Chadwick, of Battle Creek, Mich., made researches in astrology for over 40 years for the benefit of agriculture, which of course shows he was a very old man.

Charles Taylor, of Detroit, Mich., died at the age of 70.

. I, Lyman E. Stowe, the writer of these lines, am nearing 70 years old, and have been in commercial business for many years. Was a soldier during the great rebellion; am the author of many books, some of which are advertised here.

I here mention a few of the astrologers of my acquaintance.

Mr. Hodges, as his picture shows, is well along in years, but hale, hearty and as straight as an arrow. His writings in his magazine show a thoughtful, sound and brilliant mind. He jokingly said, "Do not tell my age." He probably reasoned that since one of our prominent physicians has sent forth the idea that a man should be strangled at 45, or, in other words, has lost his usefulness; thus reversing the old adage, "Old men for council, young men for war." Perhaps he would send the old men to war to get rid of them.

Mr. Hodges is one of Detroit's successful business men, often called a millionaire. The Hodges Building has been an ornament to our city for years. Mr. Hodges is also extensively engaged in various enterprises. If a millionaire it would be a blessing to our country if we had more like him. I speak of this matter to let the public see the kind of people that are interested in astrology. But, what interests us most is that Mr. Hodges edited and

## ASTROLOGY AS A SCIENCE.

published the five great astrological volumes, "Science and Key of Life." These works are unique, of great value to the casual reader and almost indispensable to the deep student of astrology.

## HENRY CLAY HODGES.

Mr. Hodges is also Editor of the Stellar Ray magazine, one of the very best magazines published for a dollar a year. We will take orders for any of the books here mentioned.

Here is MR. HODGES' GREAT QUESTION:

"SOME are born to honor, and others to dishonor; some to wealth and others to want; some in the midst of crime, ignorance and sorrow, others environed in happy conditions. When and where is the Law of Compensation applied to equalize these conditions, or why should these things be?"

## ASTROLOGY AS A SCIENCE.

MR. WHITE, of Crystal Bay, Minn., is a judge and the Editor of the Adept. A boy or a fake could not hold such positions.

Dr. MacDonald, of Binghamton, N. Y., is a well known physician and is the author of "Secrets of Astrology Revealed." This book contains one article on the rotundity of the Earth, which is worth many times the price of the book. We will furnish the book for a dollar, or it may be had of the author.

Walter H. Lewis, of Manchester, N. H., is a well known musician, composer of music and musical director of opera companies. Also the creator of the Luck Dial. We will mail this dial for a dollar or it may be had of the author.

Sullivan, of Yonkers, N. Y., must be over fifty.

Ormsby, of Chicago, is a well known author, editor and publisher, and I understand once a Government Astronomer. I have heard he is over 50.

Butler, now of California, published that wonderful book, Solar Biology (we can furnish this book for $5, and no family should be without it), 20 years ago, and his picture shows him, then, to be at least 50 years of age.

James Cross, better known as Raphael, author of the English Ephemeris I am told is over 70.

Allen Leo, editor, author and publisher, of London, England, is well along in years; and so I might go on and show that astrologers of note are men of years of experience, philosophers and men of thought and not likely to be superstitious.

Mr. White is a resident of Crystal Bay, Minn., and is the Editor of the Adept and publisher of the American Ephemeris, which is equal to, if not better than the English Ephemeris. He is also the author and publisher of many valuable works on astrology, also teacher of the science. He also fills all orders for books on Occult matters. This is not a paid ad, but is for the purpose of showing the class of

## ASTROLOGY AS A SCIENCE.

men who interest themselves in the great science. Look at the intelligence manifest in the pictures here presented and compare with those of any class of professional men. Are these not the faces of intelligent searchers after truth.

## FREDRICK WHITE,

Mr. White was born in Norton, Mass. 3 o'clock P. M., Friday, May 11, 1866. He is a typical Uranian. consequently must take to astrology. He is of American stock, light complexion, medium build, a graduate of the Boston Latin School. He served three years' apprenticeship as light machinist, and

## ASTROLOGY AS A SCIENCE.

finally became an electrician. During the panic of 1893 he found himself stranded in Chicago; here he became interested in astrology. On finding the public appreciated his work in this line he plunged deeper in the study of the occults, spending large sums of money in search of truth. Believing Minneapolis offered the best field for his labors he settled there and laid the foundation of his publishing business, finally moving to his present abiding place. Here he quickly won the confidence of the people, and although a rank Socialist he was elected Justice of the Peace, in a smart Republican town. This is certainly a good record for an astrologer or any other person.

See in our catalogue books mentioned in these biographical sketches.

### A. J. MACDONALD, M. D.

A. J. MACDONALD, M. D., Ph. D., of Binghamton, New York.

Dr. MacDonald is an astrologer that nearly every person has heard something about. He is a man of unusual intelligence, as his picture here denotes. By the name, one would almost think the doctor is fresh from Scotland, but his long American ancestry, of Scotch and Holland descent, as given in his autobiography, dispels that illusion and shows you he is one of those enterprising men who derive their superior intellect and energy from a mixed race of people.

The doctor's experience in the occults dates back to childhood and he has been a great student ever since. He has, at great expense, investigated every branch of the science; not only this, but he has done what every doctor ought to do, he has applied astrology to his medical profession.

I am sorry the want of space forbids my giving the whole of his autobiography and description of his wonder book, "Secrets of Astrology Revealed," but pshaw! what is a dollar if you are really seeking knowledge? He or any other good astrologer paid out hundreds for what they give you for a trifle. He also publishes the Planetary Hour Indicator. Send for it. Price one dollar.

## ASTROLOGY AS A SCIENCE.

ONE OF THE BEST AND MOST EARNEST IN-
VESTIGATORS of astrology in this country is Walter
H. Lewis, of Manchester, N. H.  He is the inventor
of the Luck Dial, which is a revolving disk on a bed
piece of peculiar design.  This dial is for the purpose
of getting the proper hours of the day in which to be
successful in any undertaking.  It is not only a thing
of beauty but it is a joy forever, and he predicts that
it will, eventually, be found on every business man's
table, as an indispensable article.  We can furnish it,
or it may may be had direct from Mr. Lewis.

## WALTER H. LEWIS.

Any person of good judgment can readily see by
the picture that Mr. Lewis is a man of great intelligence.  He is a musician of national reputation, so
he does not depend upon astrology for a living, but
he is fascinated with it, because of the depth as well
as the antiquity of the science.

## ASTROLOGY AS A SCIENCE.

A preacher recently asked, ironically, of a friend, referring to me: "Is he still telling fortunes for a living?"

I replied: "He is devining and fighting robbery by interest on money, two duties the Bible demands of you, and you shirk them."

The man who takes more than is justly his due, because the law gives it to him, is doubly a greater thief than he who robs you by stealth, because both take from you without your consent, and the legal thief calls to his aid those who are sworn to protect you, yet he does not share the spoils with them.

The earth is mine and the fullness thereof.—Psalms xxiv.-1, and Corinthians x.-26.

He that holds the earth or its products from his fellowman, for speculation, is robbing God as well as his fellowman.

Take thou no usury or increase.—Leviticus xxv.-36.

None but a government can make money; none but a government should lend money.

I have spoken elsewhere of my Spiritual Side of Astrology, but on finding its ramifications ran into so many other subjects, I put the bulk of it in Astrological Periodicity. To get the whole work one should read "Bible Astrology, Periodicity, What is Coming and Cosmos." The latter is only a 25c pamphlet, but is said to be the biggest little book ever published.

Lunar time 354½ days in a year, Solar time 365¼ days days. Astronomical or prophetic time 360 days "time. times and a half a time" 1260 Astronomical years.

## A FEW TESTIMONIALS.

I have never done much advertising in the line of Astrology, because I did not have to. My work has braught me all I could do without advertising. Astrologers do not get very rich writing horoscopes for a dollar each. I do more writing for a dollar than any lawyer would do for $10. I present these testimonials, not to advertise, but to show the effect of the science. I have had hundreds of fine testimonials sent me without asking. I give the following because they are all short and to the point:

Detroit, Mich., Nov. 16th, 1905.

In August, 1900, I called on Prof. Stowe for a reading. He told me I had better get my husband's life insured as he could not live to exceed seven years and was likely to die at any time.

My husband was then a strong, fleshy man, but I got his life insured, which I should not have done only for Mr. Stowe's advice.

My husband died of cancer of the bowels on Oct. 19th, 1905.

MRS. G. BELAND,
1497 Helen Ave., Detroit, Mich.

908 Union St.,
Manchester, N. H., Nov. 10, 1905.

Prof. Lyman E. Stowe,
133 Catherine St., Detroit, Mich.

My Dear Brother Stowe:

It must interest you to know how accurately your prophetic skill proves itself, so I write you to tell you that the first I knew of you was when I sent to you for your most excellent book, "The Universe," in answer to which you wrote me, in the first cf 1901, that I would soon be called west on a very important matter, of which I had not the slightest thought. On May 6th, 1901, I went west, being telegraphed for, and I afterwards met the very persons whose names you had given me, in a very strange and beneficial way.

Many of your prophecies yet remain to be fulfilled so I have future pleasant things to write you when time brings into my life.

With best wishes for the continuance of your success in Prophecy, I am ever

Yours cordially,

WALTER H. LEWIS.

Detroit, Mich., Aug. 3rd, 1906.

In 1899 I called on Prof. Lyman E. Stowe and he gave me advice I thought erroneous; and like King Charles of England, with Lilly the Astrologer, I disobeyed, and it cost me $10,000. Two years later I did the same thing again and lost again, and today ask advice I intend to follow.

W. N. MISHLRE.

Reading, Pa., 11-1-1905.

My Dear Friend Stowe:

I find the correct date of party is * * * He has been all that you warned me he would be. How marvelous that I should again be warned by you as late as July 24 about this very matter. * * * Please tell me the right and best thing to do. It is confidential, between you and me.

, Your firmest friend,

C. H. MOLLY.

I answered and soon received the following:

Reading, Pa., Nov. 8th, 1905.

Prof. Lyman E. Stowe,
133 Catherine St., Detroit, Mich.

Dear Professor:

Your findings are most wonderfully correct. Of course they should be and always must be with one well versed in the science, for if the Astronomer can figure the movements of the planets accurately

.enough to foretell the eclipse, the Astrologer should be able to figure their influences quite as readily.

I assure you I am much pleased to find that your work is very reliable and that I can depend on what you advise me, for your work satisfies me that though you do it for pay, you nevertheless put your conscience and your honor into all you do in this wonderful science. May the day soon dawn when men will live and do business more by the same, for with such directions as you are able to give them from accurate mathematical calculation *the great percentage of failures should be greatly lessened.*

Wishing you and the cause every progress,

Yours very truly,

C. F. MOLLY.

In 1901 I received an order for a horoscope of Mr. George Halsey Tuthill, of Brooklyn, N. Y. In the horoscope I told him he was about to fall heir to a large fortune.

He wrote back saying he thought the horoscope a good one, except for the idea of his falling heir to anything, as he was 70 years old and everybody dead who could leave him anything.

I wrote back: "Please let me know when you get it."

This he promised to do and it brought on a strong friendship and correspondence between us, and finally an acknowledgment that he had been notified of a small inheritance.

In November, 1905, I received the following:

"October 30, 1905.

"Dear Friend—I have received my inheritance all O. K. and it is an inheritance too far beyond my expectation. I shall go home in a few days, if assisted by other interested parties.

"Yours hastily,

"GEORGE HALSEY TUTHILL,

"169 Flatbush Ave., Brooklyn, N. Y.

Detroit, Mich., Aug. 4th, 1906.

I had a horoscope cast by Prof. L. E. Stowe which I consider very accurate, but a business matter on which I should have called for advice but which I neglected until after I had made the investment. He then told me I "let the horse be stolen and then locked the barn." Both members of the firm being in an evil cycle, they could not succeed and I have since sadly regretted that I made the investment.

MARY L. RANDALL.

## WHAT IS A HOROSCOPE?

I am often asked "What is a horoscope?"

A horoscope is a delination of character, it lets you see your self as others see you. No it does not pretend, to tell you every thing that is to take place in the future. If it did it would show you to be nothing but a machine, while the real purpose of the horoscope is to tell you what will come to you, what you should avoid and what you should take advantage of. What better can the father do for the child than to complete his education, by showing him his own nature, his good and evil periods, how to take advantage of them, and what locality, and what business he would be most successful in, and what occupation he is best adapted for.

Look at the time wasted by great men before they discovered what they were best fitted for.

A. T. Stewart was educated for the ministry; he made a failure then tried school teaching, but failed in that, then by accident he learned his proper vocation, and became one of the greatest merchant princes the world has ever known.

J. Gould failed as a storekeeper, tanner, surveyor and civil engineer, before he learned his place and became a great railroad king. Grant failed as a tanner, a farmer, merchant and banker but was one of the most successful soldiers the world ever knew. John Adams failed as a shomaker but made a brilant statesman. Josh Billings tried farming, auctioneering, and Newspaper work before he lerned that comic literature was his forte. Barnum tried fourteen different occupations before he learned he was a born showman. Paul Borghese had fourteen trades, yet starved to death.

The wealth of Rockeffeller, the success of Wanamaker, the triumphs of Edison attract and dazzle the public eye. Change positions of these men and they would prove utter failures. They met success becaus they found the business they were best adapted to. Effort or intelligence must always fail, unless applied in the proper time and place.

Now look at Ecclesiastes III-1 to 8.

1. "To every thing there is a season, and a time to every purpose under the heaven.

2. "A time to be born, and a time to die; a time to plant, and a time to pluck up that which is planted.

3. "A time to kill, and a time to heal; a time to break down, and a time to build up.

4. "A time to weep, and a time to laugh; a time to mourn, and a time to dance.

5. "A time to cast away stones, and a time to gather stones together; a time to embrace, and a time to refrain from embracing.

6. "A time to get, and a time to lose; a time to keep, and a time to cast away.

7. "A time to rend, and a time to sew; a time to keep silent, and a time to speak.

8. "A time to love, and a time to hate; a time of war, and a time of peace."

This writer was an Astrologer. If every man understood Astrology, he would know when he is likely to meet with misfortune, and so to keep still or avoid the rending, and thus avoid the mending.

In my Astrological Periodicity I show any man how to know the most of his good and evil periods, so he may take advantage of them, and by noting his periods of the past, if they are correct, he cannot help admitting the truth of those of the future.

There never was a book writen that gives so much value for $2.00 as this wonderful guide to doctors, officers of the law, or all kinds of professional men, business men and farmers, as well as to the masses of the people. It is the result of many years of hard labor.

Who would not take advantage of the knowledge which would benefit him, if he knew it?

The commercial reports claim that 95 per cent of all business men fail, sooner or later, and I will wager I can tell any man the years which his misfortune came upon him, or the years of the greatest evils of his life, as soon as I get his date of birth. Anyone sending me his place and date of birth, including the hour, if possible, with his address and $1.00 to pay my typewriter and other expenses, I will give him his characteristics, nature, what locality and occupation will be best for him, together with his good and evil periods. Shakespeare says:

"There is a tide in the affairs of man which, if taken at its flood, leads on to fortune."

Then why not take advantage of it?

## 1

SIGN of ARIES—March 21 to Apr. 19.

If born in ARIES, choose friends and business partners from those born between Feb. 15th and June 15th. Marry one born in the sign Leo, Libra, or Sagittarius.

ARIES is at the head of the 12 signs or the cosmic man, consequently is at the head of the mental triplicate, and more balanced offsprings are produced where mental signs marry with vital or neutral signs than where two of mental signs marry. It is also at the head of the fire signs, and should marry in fire signs, though they may safely marry in air signs, as air is necessary to fire, but never in a water sign, as fire and water make an explosion, and fire burns up or dries up the earth. Remember this for all fire signs. Aries people will rule the house unless they marry in a water sign, when those of the water sign will rule the house, or there will be a continual quarrel and a divorce. All signs are attracted to their polar where the greatest harmony will be found. Libra is the polar of Aries and the conservator of the vital forces, and contains an expressor of the psychics and Aries quickens this to thought. At the time of conception of an Aries person the parents were enjoying great mental and physical harmony, hence the child loves harmony, and its absence or a worry causes sickness, which first attacks the head, face, stomach, kidneys; their best remedy is quietude, rest. Being at the head of the quarter of love, their affection is great and unless happily matted, will seek desirable relations where they may be found. Their temper when aroused is hot dangerous, but they are easily appeased and quick to forgive. They take their attributes from the tribe of Gad—overcomers—activity. They love large, well-lighted rooms, music and dancing, and to excell in all they undertake, natural reasoners, originators. They cannot work well for others, as they are natural leaders and must do things their own way. They make excellent doctors, lawyers, statesmen, actors, architects, builders, designers, business men and best of psychics

**TAURUS—April 19th to May 20th.**

If born in TAURUS choose friends and business partners from those born between March 15th and July 15th. Marry one born in Virgo, Scorpio or Capricornus.

**TAURUS**

TAURUS is at the head of the earth triplicate, and of vital signs, therefore vitality is large; they are quick to recuperate. Remember this for all vital signs. They have good appetites. They should marry in earth signs, Virgo or Capricornus, though their polar is Scorpio. The men of this sign are hard to please in domestic affairs and divorces are frequent among them. Fire or water will rule them or a divorce. They may get along with air people. At the time of their conception the parents were very potent in sex life and well satisfied with life, which makes them self-willed, yet of a sympathetic nature. Temper when aroused, they look astonished, then sulk, shake the head, then go in to win regardless of consequences, yet not revengeful. Of sympathetic nature, the girls are easily led astray. These people should make their decisions when alone and stick to it. They take their destiny from the tribe of Asher. Lucky in the hour of need. Diseases first attack them in neck, throat, stomach, kidneys; liable to corpulency and dropsy in old age. They are best adapted to city life, have wonderful memories, are good in literary pursuits, good ministers, speakers, surgeons, advisers, business people, mechanics, intuitive psychic powers large.

**THE ABOVE LITTLE SKETCH**
Should be proof to the person born between the dates mentioned in the heading, that ASTROLOGY is a true science

IT IS IMPORTANT TO KNOW good and evil periods, that you may improve the good and avoid the evil

A horoscope tells you this, also your GEMS, COLORS, RULING STAR, DISEASES most subject to, what best ADAPTED to, LOCALITY BEST for you and many other things

SIGN of GEMINI—May 20 to June 21.

If born in GEMINI choose friends or business partners from those born between April 15th and August 15th. Marry one born in Libra, Sagittarius or Aquarius.

GEMINI is at the head of the air triplicate and of the neutral signs. Though the love nature is strong, they hide their affection, and should marry in a neutral sign. As earth and water make mud, and fire dries up the earth, so does air. Air also either dries up the water or lashes it to fury, yet water will rule, and they should marry in Sagittorus, its polar or acquareus or libra, though air will get along with any of the signs better than fire, water or earth will do. This answers for all of the air signs. They take their destiny from the tribe of Isachor, and are natural students. At the time of their conception their parents were very active and restless, hence Gemini people are of a restless nature, wanting something they can't tell what, oft times a combative feeling and vague imagining of evil, yet active and want to be doing something all of the time; oftimes inconsistent, liable to nervous disturbances. Sickness is first felt in the shoulders, arms, hands, lungs. Like Aries and Taurus peopel, they are inclined to drink, and the men are dressy and proud and overbearing. Both sexes love to appear better than they are. They love knowledge and make good musicians, teachers, speakers and business people, but do not like drudgery.

## SIGN of CANCER—June 21 to July 22.

If born in CANCER choose friends and business partners from those born between May 15th and September 15th. Marry one born in Scorpio, Capriocrnus or Pisces.

CANCER stands at the head of the quarter of wealth, and the water triplicate. Enough has been said to show that those of a water sign should marry in their own sign, Scorpio or Pices, though Capricornus is the polar of Cancer and is the generalizer in business plans and Cancer in the home relations; hence harmony is best assured, whether slow or quick to show temper, and Cancer is generally quick when fully aroused. They are good haters, and even if they ever forgive, it always comes up in the mind at the first provocation and they get even sooner or later. This is the case with all water signs. At the time of their conception their parents were over-anxious for children and the pleasures of married life. Consequently Cancer people are great lovers of home and make themselves slaves to their children, doing everything instead of making a help of the child. Their destiny springs from the tribe Zeublon, love of home and business ability, good money-makers, yet at times suddenly leave a good business with little or no reason, so seldom attain a very high aim, yet are often persistent in executing their plans. Disease first attacks them in the breast, stomach and kidneys. They should be careful of their digestion. Though good mechanics, they are best adapated to trading or business pursuits.

If born in LEO choose friends and business partners from those born between June 15th and Oct. 15th. Marry one born in Sagittarius, Aquarius or Aries.

LEO—July 22d to August 23d.

LEO people are of hot temper, though easily appeased and are not revengeful. They will harmonize with their polar aquarius, but will live happily, and produce the best families when they marry in Aries. Their destinies are from the tribe of Joseph—love and unconventionality. Their weakness is their love nature; in consequence easily misled. They are liable to imitate others and jump at conclusions too quickly. Their nature springs from a deep soul love by their parents at time of their conception. They live in an ideal world, in great hopes, yet are courageous and look out for themselves. Disease first attacks their heart and head. They are observant and law abiding; too liable to appeal to the law and waste good money. Children in this sign should be governed by positive law and looked after on account of their strong sex and love nature. These people will be found in every pursuit of life, and are equally successful in whatever they adapt themselves to, as they choose their occupation by intuition; but they are natural geniuses and often inventors.

SIGN of VIRGO—Aug. 22 to Sept. 23.

If born in VIRGO choose friends and business partners from those born between July 15th and November 15th. Marry one born in Capricornus, Pisces or Taurus.

VIRGO belongs to the earth and neutral signs, as before mentioned, and will be attracted to and harmonize with Pices people, though they should marry in Taurus, Gemini, Capricornus or Sagitterus. At the time of their conception the parents were in a soul-loving nature and intent on making themselves happy; hence Virgo people are loving, yet selfish. They are of a jealous nature, and at the least in harmony sulk and cannot eat. Disease attacks them in the bowels, stomach and head. Their destinies arise from the tribe of Benjamin—self-reliance, selfishness. Children are peculiar about their diet. Their natural instinct tells them what is best for them; so do not restrain them except in quantity, as children of this sign are hard to raise until after they pass their sixth year. They are natural chemists, make excellent and rapid proofreaders, good in colors, hence good artists. They are natural students and lovers of music, often good singers, but lose their voice very young.

VIRGO ♍

SIGN of LIBRA—Sept. 23 to Oct. 23.

If born in Libra, choose friends and business partners from those born between August 15th and December 15th. Marry one born in Sagittarius, Aquarius, or Aries.

LIBRA is of the mental air signs, and, as stated in Aries, is the polar of Aries and harmonizes best with Aries, next with Aquarius or Leo in marriage. Their temper is like all air signs, quick, flashy and quick over it and sorry for giving offense—apt to ask pardon, and later in life overcome and show no temper. They should never marry in a neutral sign, as their starved affections will kill them. Their destinies are from the tribe of Reuben—dignity and psychic power. Like Aries people, unless well mated will seek desirable relations where they can be found. At the time of their conception the parents were not pulling together. One was confiding, the other careless, if not actually false. So Libra people are always looking for something better and are very hopeful, yet subject to spells of unaccountable sadness. Disease first attacks them in back, rines, head, stomach and nerves. You seldom find them very high or very low in the walks of life, though they are liable to gamble, and if they lose in stake or business they never lose hope. It is advisable that they carry out their first decisions in all matters. They are not good reasoners, but are nearly always right in their decisions by intuition. They will judge a horse accurately, telling what ails him, but cannot tell how they gained their knowledge; in fact they cannot give a good reason for anything. They are affectionate and positive in their likes and dislikes. Children should be trained to control their sex nature, which is strong, but quickly becomes normal as they increase in age. They are good in about the same lines as Virgo people, but a little better mechanics and more liable to speculation. They are at the head of the quarters of wealth.

SCORPIO—October 23d to November 22d.

If born in SCORPIO chooose business partners and trusted friends from those born between September 15th and January 15th. Marry one born in the sign Pisces, Taurus or Cancer.

SCORPion ♏

SCORPio ♏

SCORPIO belongs to the water and vital signs, and should marry in Cancer or Picus, though attracted to its polar Taurus it would be bad for the Tavrus person, and on account of the stubborn will of both signs and the jealousy of both natures, if once aroused, would surely result in murder. They recover from illness very quickly., and disease in youth are colds mainly or such disease as children are subject to, but later in life diease is first felt in the urinary organs, heart, or stomach. Their destiny arises from the tribe of Simeon—self will, hot temper, never forgetting an injury, even though they forgive.

At te time of their conception, their parents were not pulling together as well as they ought to, yet, had a desire to put the best side out; therefore the children are exacting, though kindhearted, often spending money freely, but generally get more for it than most people, for they are very good financiers, make the best foremen, superintendents and managers, as they live up to their agreements and expects others to do the same.

They are very witty, and are excellent company.

SIGN of SAGITTARIUS—Nov. 22 to Dec. 21.

If born in SAGITTARIUS choose friends and business partners from those born between October 15th and February 15th. Marry one born in Aries, Gemini or Leo.

ARCHER.

SAGITTARUS

SAGITTARUS closes the fire triplicate, of neutral sign, hide their affection, and those only of a similar nature should marry with them. Gemini is their polar and well suited to them, as Sagittarus is the physical expressor, server and protector, while Gemini is the artificer and intellectual expressor. They will do well with either of the fire signs, but the affection of Leo or Aries must starve or seek solace elsewhere. Disease first attacks the sciatic nerves. "Oh, my hips ache so;" also chest, lungs and kidneys. Their destiny springs from the tribe of Levi—high temper and jealousy, impulsive and hold hate longer than any of the fire signs. They hate anything hidden or secret, too quick to decide, are of one thought, one idea at a time, yet they are far-seeing, their minds continually running ahead. They will lie rather than give up when they are wrong. They are apt to make a good story better, and so often are accused of falsehood where none was intended. They are natural mathematicians, good business people and good servers. If you find a person who says "I have no such a high temper," just ask him if he does not take some pride in overcoming. As people grow older they overcome to a greater or less extent and add so much to their honor.

**SIGN of CAPRICORNUS—Dec. 21 to Jan. 20.**

If you were born in CAPRICORNUS choose trusted friends or business partners from those born between November 15th and March 15th. Marry one born in Virgo, Taurus or Cancer.

CAPRICORNUS is the head of the quarter of labor and last of the earth and mental signs, is polarized and harmonizes with cancer, may marry in Taurus person, and on account polarized and harmonious Taurus or Virgo or an air sign. Their destiny arises from the tribe of Judah, organization and business. Their temper is of the earth signs, generally sulky.

Like libra people, if they do not marry young, are liable not to marry at all. The women generally marry men much older than themselves. At the time of their conception their parents were in great expectation and hopefully looking to large speculation and business enterprises, hence these people are hopeful and liable to risk everything and spend the last dollar and impoverish themselves to keep in the swim. They love a business that gives them a sitting posture, though it is bad for them, and activity is their nature, making good agriculturists, contractors and traveling salesmen, as disease attacks the knees and kidneys, rheumatism and gout set in unless they lead active lives. They are lovers of literature, art and education. Their sex passions are strong; soul affection weak.

SIGN of AQUARIUS—Jan. 20 to Feb. 19.

If born in AQUARIUS choose trusted friends or business partners from those born between December 15th and April 15th. Marry one born in Gemini, Leo or Libra.

 AQUARIUS is the last of the air triplicate. Its polar is Leo, though it is attracted to Libra, Aries, Gemini and Taurus, which are its best signs for marriage. Temper, flashy, quick over and sorry for giving offense; they generally overcome and show no temper at all. Their destiny springs from the tribe of Dan, which is a contradiction of nature. It is called the highest and lowest of the twelve signs, as they soar very high and often stoop very low. They are reasoners and natural skeptics. Their minds are wholly in the useful, good judges of character, good in business life, and take great interest in public affairs. Their sphere is in city life, and business that requires great activity. They have great controlling power with the eye. At time of their conception their parents were active in business that required watchfulness of character of others. They are of the active, nervous temperament. Disease is first felt in calves of legs and kidneys.

SIGN of PISCES—Feb. 19 to March 21.

If born in PISCES choose friends and business partners from those born between January 15th and June 15th. Marry one born in Cancer, Virgo or Scorpio.

SIGN of PISCES—Feb. 19 to March 21.

If born in PISCES choose friends and business partners from those born between January 15th and June 15th. Marry one born in Cancer, Virgo or Scorpio.

**PISCES**

PICES is the last of the water signs; is always revengeful, but generally subdued to refusing all intercourse with the party of their dislike. Their polar is Virgo, but should marry in Virgo or in the water signs. Sickness attacks them in feet, head and lungs. Their destiny is from the tribe of Naphtali—activity—studious nature. At time of conception their parents were in a struggling, antagonistic nature, hence they are of a restless, nervous, ofttimes sad disposition; good clairvoyants or clear seers, faithful adherents to the marriage vow. They make useful accountants and good business people, finest of horticulturists and agriculturists. They are always active, yet cry out, "Oh, my feet ache so!" They are natural philanthropists and reformers, though are apt to accept measures as a reform act without giving it proper weight.

CPSIA information can be obtained
at www.ICGtesting.com
Printed in the USA
LVHW061244050820
661838LV00009B/112